The Salvation Army
and
the
Churches

Authors whose writings are included

Mrs. General William Booth
General Bramwell Booth
General Arnold Brown
General Frederick Coutts
General Wilfred Kitching
General Albert Orsborn
General Clarence D. Wiseman
Lt.-Colonel Harry Dean
Major William Wilson
Mrs. Ballington Booth
Rev. Thomas Phillips, D.D.

Other books by the same author:

At the Center of the Circle
G.S.R.
O Boundless Salvation
The Privilege of all Believers
The Salvationist and the Atonement
Women in The Salvation Army
The Salvation Army and the Children

The Salvation Army and the Churches

*An anthology of selected articles
by Salvationist authors, past and present,
on the relationship of The Salvation Army
to the established Christian Churches.*

**Compiled by
Commissioner John D. Waldron (R)**

The Salvation Army
Literary Department
145 West 15th Street
New York, N.Y. 10011

ISBN. 0-89216-064-0

Copyright © 1986
The Salvation Army
All Rights Reserved

Published by: The Salvation Army Literary Department
145 West 15th Street
New York, N.Y. 10011

Printed in the United States of America

Table of Contents

Foreword

Anthologists and compilers are a rare species, and thinkers, writers, speakers and students owe them an immense debt. Their labor saves ours. They are "discerners." They relieve us of the tedious process of evaluating this or that as worthy of consideration, having themselves carefully sifted the wheat from the chaff in order to leave a residue that will merit our attention.

Compilation is a field in which Commissioner John Waldron has specialized, as the list of his other productions will impressively attest. The subject he has chosen for this publication is one of prime interest to those who want to know their location in the ecumenical vineyard, or what their relationship is to other members of the Body of Christ in the world.

The essays included could, in the main, be regarded as positional statements, so far as The Salvation Army is concerned. The names of no fewer than seven international leaders of the Movement are by-lines over ten of the chapters. And seeing Catherine Booth, whose words lead the way into this mini-library, is regarded as one of the Army's founders, the total of contributing leaders goes up to eight.

The articles span the lifetime of the Army, and though the world William Booth knew has evolved beyond his visionary imaginings, the subject which occupied his wife's perceptive mind a century ago is still intriguing and important.

The best thanks we can offer Commissioner Waldron for his painstaking research is to see that those who need enlightenment on the subject of *The Salvation Army and the Churches* have this useful tool placed in their hand.

Arnold Brown
General (R)

Introduction

Is The Salvation Army a church? A social agency? A civic organization? In a sense, it is a combination of all of these. In another sense, it is none of them. It is an Army, unique in ecclesiastical and sociological history, an Army of Christian soldiers mobilized to fight the evils that would deface the image of God in His creation.

At its inception, the infant Movement made no claim to be a social agency. The ministry of the early Christian Mission was entirely evangelistic. Out of its Christian compassion grew increased efforts to serve humanity's material needs. This ultimately found its fruition in the Founder's book, *In Darkest England and the Way Out,* published a quarter of a century after the Army was born. But performing acts of charity is not its primary purpose.

Until its more mature years, the Army did not have the standing in society to be considered a civic organization, although it is now widely recognized as a community force to be reckoned with. But that is not the Army's basic reason for existence.

From the moment that William Booth started preaching in a Quaker tent in East London, the essential heartbeat of the Army has been found in the Gospel of Christ. Its pioneers proclaimed that the blood of Jesus Christ cleansed from all sin, and proved it as they gave themselves in happy abandon to the ministry of soul-winning.

Salvationists sang hymns, read the Scriptures, subscribed to a creed, established congregations, preached the Gospel, erected places of worship—in other words, did the things usually associated with the Church.

Why, then, was the Army not recognized as part of the Church Universal by many religious leaders? Was it because it adopted unconventional methods? Or did not observe the sacraments? Or because it ordained women?

What was the attitude of the Booths toward the churches of their day? Is it true that Booth warned his people against being "churchy"? The structured church of the 1860s in Great Britain was often sterile, lacking in compassion for the poor, and stereotyped in its worship. Booth cried out for freedom in worship, innovative methods, and the grace of caring.

In our day, do people misunderstand the Army's ultimate reason for existence because they see only our most visible—and eminently praiseworthy—network of social services and civic leadership?

In this anthology, you will find some of the answers from those who founded the Movement, as well as those who guided it through the years until the present day. Here is Catherine Booth, declaring that we are "not diverse from the churches." Here are the astute leaders of the 20th century as they struggle with the question of the Army's identity with the conciliar churches.

To return to the questions in the first paragraph, "What is the Army?" and "What is its function?" may we reverently paraphrase the Apostle Paul: "Now there remaineth these three: The Salvation Army ministers to the poor, it works to uplift society, and it preaches the Gospel of Christ, but the greatest of these is preaching the Gospel." Is not this the primary task of the Church Universal? It certainly is the primary task of The Salvation Army!

1

Are We a Church?

by Clarence D. Wiseman

From *The Officer,* October 1976. Published by
The Salvation Army, International Headquarters, London.

PEOPLE often ask me, "What is The Salvation Army?"
One would expect such a question in countries where we
recently "opened fire," but it also arises where we have
served for many years. In fact, I know Salvationists who
appear perplexed about our identity. Should they call their
corps a church? If not, why not? Where does the Army fit into
the ecclesiastical pattern?

Now and again I am reminded that we have never developed a theology of the Church. The traditional retort to
such a comment is that we have been too busy doing the
Lord's work to take time to think seriously about our precise
position in His "Body." Not that this article lays claim to taking
even one small step toward such a theology! It is simply a
few random reflections of the theme—no more, no less.
Some day someone will tackle the task.

In the beginning we were a *mission.* That is how we
started. "When I saw East London in the year 1864-65," the
Founder recalled on one occasion, "I found resolution to try
something on the line of a perpetual revival, and so started

the East London Revival Mission." Clearly, it was a mission, not a church.

Even after the change of name to The Salvation Army in 1878, he continued to insist that the Movement was not a church. It was now an *Army.* "It was not my intention to create another sect ... we are not a church. We are an Army—an Army of Salvation."

When a wave of charitable sympathy for the Army swept Britain after the publication in 1890 of *In Darkest England and the Way Out,* the churches were prepared to see the new development in the religious life of the country as a "regiment of the great Army in the forces of Christianity that is making a way and a highway for the coming of the King." But insistence we were not a church continued.

There was an understandable explanation for this. Had not the young William Booth run foul of Church authorities when he resigned as a local preacher in order to devote himself to personal hand-to-hand combat for souls in the open-air? His membership ticket in the Wesleyan Connexion was withdrawn; he was accused of being a rebel. It is worth noting that about this time deep internal controversies were rocking the Methodist Church!

Many years later the Founder recalled this episode. He said the agitation that deprived him of membership was really over ecclesiastical questions for which he cared not a penny! Is it possible this experience helped color his future attitude?

In the mid-nineteenth century, churches were shunned by the poor. Lord Shaftesbury asserted that not two percent of the working men of London went to any place of worship. Furthermore, revivalism of William Booth's kind was actually discouraged in England by the unsympathetic reaction of the churches—though there were exceptions. Robert Sandall, in the first volume of *The History of The Salvation Army,* points out that the governing bodies of the principal Methodist churches were opposed to revivalism. He also quotes from an established church magazine which attacked the attempt to reach the churchless masses by holding religious meetings in theatres, lamenting that the evil of such activities "will remain in the lowered estimate of the dignity and solemnity of the Most High!"

Probably the Army's compassion and good works, so like the early Franciscans, has prompted some people to see us as a modern *religious order.* During the Second World War, I met the venerable head of the Franciscan monastery in the Garden of Gethsemane. Affectionately, he described the Army in precisely these terms—he called it "an Order within the Protestant Church."

There are Salvationists in some parts of Scandinavia who up till now appear to have had little difficulty reconciling membership in a State-church with membership in the Army. It must be said that this duality has in no way diminished their devotion, but it does raise an important question: should the Army in such circumstances be looked upon as a religious order?

It is a well-known fact that in not a few countries the very name "Salvation Army" evokes the image of a *social service agency* that succours the poor and helps the distressed. How often have we heard, "I always give to the Army. They help people the churches do not reach."

As early as the 1904 International Congress in London, William Booth, with rare perceptivity, warned that this very thing might happen. He admitted there were people even then who "thought the Army was a system for the administration of poor relief, or a mission for the employment of the unfortunate."

It was as part of the same address that he made a quite startling statement in view of previous denials that the Army was a church. "The Army," he declared, "is part of the living Church of God—a great instrument of war in the world, engaged in deadly conflict with sin and fiends." Though he did not say the Army was a church in the denominational sense, it was quite clear he considered it to be part of the universal Church, the Body of Christ!

This theme was taken up even more positively by his son and successor, General Bramwell Booth, who, incidentally, subtly varied a number of positions adopted earlier on, all part of the evolution of the Movement. In *Echoes and Memories,* published in 1925, he wrote:

> There is one Church ... And being one, yet it is to be for all people and all classes. In the Church of Christ there is neither Greek nor Jew, circumcision nor uncircumcision, Barbarian, Scythian, bond nor free; but Christ is all and in all. Of this, the Great Church of the Living God, we claim, and have ever claimed, that we of The Salvation Army are an integral part and element—a living, fruit-bearing branch in the True Vine. ... And our officers are ... ministers in the Church of God, having received diversities of gifts, but the one Spirit—endowed by His grace, assured by His guidance, confirmed by His Word, and commissioned by the Holy Ghost to represent Him to the whole world.

The picture now begins to take shape. We are still a *mission.* The sixth General, Albert Orsborn, said within comparatively recent times, "We are *not* a church—we are a permanent mission to the unconverted."

Those who heard him say this repeatedly, knew exactly what he meant. The Army must never cease to be a mission to the unsaved, a potent revival force in the world. Failure at this point would mean abdication from one of the major purposes for which God brought us into existence. The mission stamp must always be upon us!

But we are more than a mission—we are an *Army.* God's shocktroops. We can be no other. Our destiny is written large in our name. We are structured to cope with the changing demands of spiritual warfare, gifted with capacity for quick decisions when needed, and mobility to meet emergencies; our officers and soldiers are ready and willing to serve "for Jesus' sake." All this is of God.

Where the concept of the religious order has allowed people to be loyal Salvationists though associated with a

4

State-church, then surely we should not deny it a place in our growing composite picture of The Salvation Army, provided, of course, that the Movement possesses freedom and autonomy necessary to maintain its identity and function.

The grace of flexibility without surrender of essentials has been given us by the Holy Spirit, a pragmatism firmly bound by enveloping principles and doctrines! There is no reason why such flexibility should not continue to influence the Army if we allow the free wind of the Spirit constantly to blow through us. Openness to the Spirit is surely more creative than narrow dogmatisms that try to put up the shutters when God strives to show us a new thing! Precedents are helpful as guiding lines, never as invariable laws.

One must confess to an inner disquiet when people view the Army only as a *social service agency*. But we understand the reason. Knowing something of the Army's good works, but probably perceiving little of its religious life or motivation, they quite naturally think of us as they see us. Where this happens I trust tactful steps are taken to correct such an imbalanced perspective—though without any apology for our social ministry. Social concern is inherent, given by God. In this we but follow, and must ever follow, the compassionate example of our Lord Himself.

It appears, in the light of all I have said, that we are a permanent *mission* to the unconverted and a caring *social service movement;* in some places we assume the features of a *religious order.* These various aspects exist within the God-given shape of an *Army,* the world-wide Army of Salvation! Can all these elements be subsumed under the generic designation *church?*

With a few exceptions, I think most authorities would agree with us that the Army is part of the living Church of God—the Body of Christ. I believe also the Army can be truthfully described as a "church" in the more circumscribed, denominational sense of the word.

Let us start with our legal foundation. The first of the five

5

documents that together determine the present constitution of The Salvation Army is a Deed Poll (that is, a deed made and executed by one person only) dated August 7, 1878. It states that "a number of people were formed into a community or society ... for the purpose of enjoying religious fellowship and in order to continue and multiply ... efforts ... to bring under the gospel those who were not in the habit of attending any place of worship by preaching in the open air, in tents, theatres, music halls and other places and by holding religious services or meetings...."

Cumbersome though the language is, surely this statement goes a long way toward establishing the Army as a church in the legal sense of the term. Legal standing was confirmed in the United States during the Second World War when it was found necessary to determine if the Army was a church and its officers bona fide ministers of religion within the requirement of certain Acts of the U.S.A. Congress. The outcome of lengthy, detailed investigation by competent experts led to the unequivocal conclusion that in the eyes of American law the Army *is* a church, and that "all commissioned officers of The Salvation Army, as they are now constituted, are regular or duly ordained ministers of religion...."

Do I hear someone interrupting the argument, suggesting that a legal definition is all right in its place, but the history of churches reveals that much more ecclesiastical furniture than the Army possesses is required to qualify as a "church"? Unfortunately, when we examine the history of the churches, the story is strewn with so many conflicting claims that it becomes difficult to discern one clear pattern. What one group deems sufficient another counts inadequate. Serious attempts to comprehend the subtle theological nuances associated with controversial subjects like baptism, the Lord's Supper, apostolic succession, papal infallibility and so on, thrust one into the middle of such an ecclesiastical jungle that one can understand the Founder's hesitation about calling an Army a church!

However, there is no doubt that the Army stands within the mighty spiritual movement that started with Christ and His Apostles and has continued unbroken to this day, and will continue through time and eternity. The faith of the Army is the faith affirmed through the ages in the great creeds of the Church. The discipline of the Army is inspired by New Testament teaching. The worship of the Army is in the name of the risen Lord, and in harmony with His words: "But the hour cometh, and now is, when the true worshippers shall worship the Father in spirit and in truth: for the Father seeketh such to worship Him. God is a Spirit: and they that worship Him must worship Him in spirit and in truth" (John 4:23, 24).

Some might argue that, as the Army does not observe the sacraments (though it does not forbid their observance by its members), it is not a church. Yet others might claim that because its officers are not duly ordained by bishops who stand within the apostolic succession their ministry is invalid. These and other contentions bring to my memory a fine paragraph in a book I picked up recently in India, *The Nature and the Calling of the Church* by William Stewart, of Serampore College, published in 1958.

He points out quite rightly that Christians of various denominations are fully justified in seeking to express the orderly life of their church by the reverent use of the means which they are sure God has given to them, such as the Scriptures, the creeds, the sacraments, the ministry. Then he goes on:

> But what they are not *justified in doing* is to take any of these means, or even all together, and make them a final test by which to pass judgement on whether or not others are within the Catholic (Universal) Church. If they are "in Christ" we cannot possibly say they are not in the church, and the very fact that there are, for

7

instance, some Christians who do not use the sacraments, but whom we must acknowledge that He has blessed, forbids us to deny that they are "members of Christ." The one test which He has given is "by their fruits ye shall know them" (Matthew 7:20).

If the above statement is true, and I believe it is, only one further step is required to say that a group of Christians like Salvationists, banded together in fellowship, worship and service in Jesus' name and admittedly part of the Body of Christ, should also be seen as one among the numerous groups that call themselves "churches"!

The Salvation Army is one of these churches whose members, born again of the Holy Spirit and obedient to the heavenly vision, constitute the great Church of God. But let us never forget its distinctive qualities, its forthright evangelism, its joy, the absence of formalism, its simplicity of worship with opportunities for free prayer and testimony, its caring concern for people whatever their need! If these distinctions are eroded we should cease to be the kind of Movement God intended us to be.

Just one further word. In the quest for our particular position in the modern ecclesiastical pattern let us never lose sight of the more important position we hold in relation to the risen Lord, without which all else would be in vain. He describes it most beautifully in Matthew 18:20: "For where two or three are gathered together in My name, there am I in the midst of them."

The precious companies of redeemed soldiers of God gathered together in Salvation Army corps give credence to the claim that we are both a church and a part of the universal Church. These companies have within them the germ and the power of all religious possibilities simply because He, of whose Body they are a small part, stands in their midst as He stands in the midst of all other groups of true believers. What more can we ask?

8

2

The Salvation Army and Its Relation to the Churches

by Catherine Booth

From *The Salvation Army in Relation to the Church and State, and other addresses,* published by The Book Depot of The Salvation Army, London, 1883.

TO those who were with us last week it will not be necessary to repeat the harrowing details of the condition of the masses, but only to beg of you to bear those facts in mind in considering our relation to the churches. Let me add also the terrible fact, ascertained by carefully taken statistics, that prior to the commencement of our operations, ninety per cent of these masses never entered church, chapel, or mission hall! Surely everybody who believes in any kind of religion must see the awful necessity for some extraneous and irregular agency, adapted to reach this continent of dark, indifferent, infidel souls!

Firstly: *We are not antagonistic to the churches.* Anyone would suppose we were, from the adverse criticisms we get from Christian papers. This is quite a mistake; it is not so in reality. They do give us credit for having a great deal of the charity which endures all things, or else they must have expected we should have been driven into open opposition; but we do not intend to be. As the General said to the present Archbishop of Canterbury, when speaking to him

9

about The Salvation Army: "We think that we have a claim upon your sympathy, because we do not seek to justify our existence, by finding fault with you." No; we do not attack either organizations or individuals. All we find fault with, is SIN; but if some people in the churches find that the cap fits, we cannot help it. It is not with the Church, or the good and godly people in it, that we find fault. It is one of our most emphatic instructions to our officers: "It is not your business to go and find fault with other people. Rejoice in all the good done, by whomsoever it is done. Be glad whenever you find a good man or woman at work for God, and for the salvation of the people. Never try to find a hole in their coat, or pull them to pieces. Mind your own business, which is seeking and saving the lost." We have acted upon this ourselves from the beginning.

Secondly: *Neither are we indifferent to the opinion or sympathy of the churches.* We desire and value, as I think all workers for humanity must, the sympathy and prayer and assistance of all good men. We care very little about creeds. God has shown us that all forms are very much alike, when the spirit has gone out of them.

We believe that God cares very little about our sectarian differences and divisions. The great main thing is the love of God and the service of humanity; and when we find people actuated by this motive, we love them by whatever name they are called. We do not set at nought their opinions. Friends would little imagine how carefully we have considered their suggestions. It is not very long since a minister said he had found out that "we were only playing at soldiering." These things of course are very painful to us, after my dear husband's thirty-five years' toil for the masses, and very much anxious thought, study, and prayer as to the best way to advance the Master's kingdom. We have done the very best we could, and we must leave such criticisms to rectify themselves, or rather for God and time to rectify them.

People think that we have adopted these plans and measures because of some personal predilection. They forget that we had to fight our way out of traditionalism and conventionalism just the same as they would have had to do if they had been laid under the same painful necessity. We were resolved on reaching the people, and therefore we have accepted the only conditions possible under the circumstances.

Thirdly: *Neither are we diverse from the churches in the great fundamental doctrines of Christianity.* We have not adopted any of the new gospels of these times. We have not given up any of the fundamental doctrines of Christianity, such as the Fall, the universal call to repentance, justification by faith through Jesus Christ, a life of obedience, heaven and hell.

Then you say, *Wherein is the difference?* Well, the main difference is in our *aggressiveness.* This is manifested in several ways. The Bishop of Durham, the learned Dr. Lightfoot, says: "The Salvation Army has at least recalled us to the lost ideal of the work of the Church—the universal compulsion of the souls of men." Yes, we have been teaching our own people first, and through their influence others, that by the help and grace of God such measure of influence and power may be brought to bear upon men as may lead them to salvation. We teach them that we are to compel men to come in, that we are to seek by our own individual power and by the power of the Holy Ghost in us to persuade men, that the Gospel idea of preaching is not merely laying the truth before men, for the exercise of their intellectual faculties; but that a teacher and saviour has something more to do than this—that he ought to be possessed of sufficient Divine influence to thrust his message in upon the heart, to make the soul realize and feel his message. This is our great characteristic—pressing the Gospel upon the attention of men.

11

We have not only to a large extent resuscitated this *idea,* but by the power of God (we claim nothing of ourselves) we have also raised a force of men and women who are now *working it out,* to an extent that no people preceding us, so far as Church history shows, have ever conceived of—a people who have a more comprehensive idea of their responsibility, both as individuals and as an organization, than ever existed in the world before. There have existed exceptional men, many, thank God; but *as an organization* there is no record since the days of the Apostles of a body that has so compassed the Divine idea, all its members being taught to make all the other objects and aims of life subservient to the one grand purpose of preaching the Gospel to every creature, and striving to win every soul with whom they come in contact to its salvation.

The same Spirit also that has awakened us to this continued and persistent activity, has also directed us as to the course in which it was to be directed. This same Divine Spirit has directed our attention to the moral cesspools of the country. We need not have gone to them. It was our own free choice. Many people do not know this; but we had no more necessity to do it than any minister in this room. Our path embraced all the comforts and prospects of a successful ministerial career; but as by miracle (I cannot account for it in any other way) we were led into this particular description of work.

The General was led in the first instance, more especially, to contemplate these waste masses, this continent of souls, it seemed, without any light, life, or power, left untouched, confessedly by our bishops, clergy, ministers, and philanthropists, without any humanizing, much less to say Christianizing influences. My dear husband was led especially to the East of London without any idea beyond that of a local work. God showed him that between the churches and the working classes, as a rule, there was a great gap; he saw that there was needed some instrumentality that would

12

come between the two, and take hold of this lower stratum, which, in the great majority of cases, was uncared-for and unthought-of; and he set himself to do it in the East of London.

God so wonderfully blessed him that the work soon began to grow of its own aggressive and expansive force. Some of the greatest reprobates in London got converted in the East London Mission. They came for seven, ten, and fifteen miles to those services, to look at "Bill," "Bob," or "Jack," some fighting, dog-fancying, or pigeon-flying companion, who was reported to have been saved on the previous Sunday—and some of these got caught also. They were changed, transformed, and put into their right minds; and immediately became anxious for the salvation of their fellows. Some of these came to my husband and said there were whole streets of working men in their neighborhoods who never went to a place of worship—could they not do something for them? Could they not open little mission rooms and set to work to try to save them?

In these early days we had no funds or helpers except a few voluntary working men, the richest of them not earning more than thirty shillings a week. My husband would say: "I have no funds, and I have nobody to be responsible; but if you can get anybody's kitchen or an old dancing saloon or penny gaff, I will get some of my working men to come and help you on Sundays, and you must do the rest yourselves." Thus, little missions at Poplar, Canning-Town, and other places were opened; and in this way the Christian Mission has grown into The Salvation Army!

It grew because of the Divine life that was in it. We could not help it, even if we had desired to do so. All life must grow and develop; if you cramp it—shut it in—it will die. If it is to become powerful, you must let it have room to express itself. The Salvation Army has grown so fast because it has been allowed to have free course! God has helped us to raise a gigantic spiritual force in the land, which is carrying out the idea of the "compulsion of souls." We have, today, something like 1,200 officers of The Salvation Army, or what you would call evangelists—paid officers; and when I say paid, I only mean supported. We do not reckon to *pay anybody*, not even our staff officers. We have officers on our staff who a little while ago held positions worth from £200 to £800 a year, only receiving enough to keep themselves and their families in a moderate degree of comfort, who have made all sorts of pecuniary sacrifices in order to become Salvation Army officers; and we have many others waiting, who are ready at this moment to renounce lucrative businesses and situations to come and throw themselves into this work. We had, some months ago, 20,000 voluntary public speakers, unpaid, that is, men and women whom their captain could call upon at a moment's notice for any kind of service: ready to spring into the gap, tell their experience, pray, march, go to prison, or anything else necessary for the salvation of their fellow-men.

At an Exeter Hall meeting not long ago, my husband had called upon what was once a poor rag-picker, a woman who was rescued from drink and depravity, though a woman of good natural ability, and a woman who, when her husband was worsted in a fight, he used to hand over his opponent to her, and she could manage him. This woman got converted, and when she reached home at ten o'clock at night, she dragged her three little children out of bed, and setting them on their knees round a chair, said: "Your mother never prayed with you before, but she will do it now." After such a beginning it is not surprising she succeeded in getting them converted, and in inspiring them with the love of God and of souls, so that they have become perfect heroines in this Army. My husband called upon this woman on the Exeter Hall platform, without a moment's notice, to speak, and she did so. An influential clergyman said to me afterwards in the committee room: "It is perfectly astonishing. There is not one in a hundred of us could do as well as that woman did if we were called upon at a minute's notice."

Oh, yes; it is astonishing what, by the power of God in these people, they can accomplish. We had months ago 20,000 people of that type, and now near double that number, of course not all so gifted as that one, who speak nightly, and two or three times on a Sabbath in the open air, who have literally to fight with wild beasts, and to encounter the biggest rowdies and cut-throats in the country. They button-hole these men, and talk to them with tears in their eyes. They often kneel down in the snow or mud and pray and plead with them, in *their way;* and it suits them much better than ours would, because it matches their nature better.

You must not think, however, that these trained speakers represent our troops. Oh, no; we have thousands of soldiers, most of them occasional speakers. These only represent our reliable open-air troops; but we are raising a mightier force than these, and God is showing us by circumstances the want of other kinds of officers. We have a new order of officers called "Sergeants," who come between the corps and the paid officers; and we hope soon to have a force of these who will systematically visit every public-house in the country, and scavenge houses of worse repute still, who will make it their duty to scavenge the back alleys, and worst places of resort in the nation, irrespective of abuse or ill-usage. We are raising such people. God is doing it through our instrumentality.

Is this any more than needs to be done? Nay, will anything less than this determined hand-to-hand fight with evil, serve to stem the tide of sin and demoralization which threatens our national life? What a long time the Church has been singing—I don't want to reflect on anybody—but how long has the Church been singing:

> "Onward, Christian soldiers,
> Marching as to war,
> With the Cross of Jesus
> Going on before"?

How long have we been singing:

> "Am I a soldier of the Cross?"

And yet how little hand-to-hand fighting with sin and the devil! God has, however, taught us better, and we are determined to carry the battle into the very strongest fortresses of the enemy.

A further difference between us and the majority of the churches is, the resuscitation of the *supernatural,* of the Divine. *Here, I think, is our real power.* We do not underestimate intellect. God forbid. We have developed, as somebody said the other day, a large amount of intellectual power amongst the masses; because, you see, God's gifts are far more generously and impartially distributed than we are apt to imagine. Polish is not power; education is not intellect. We have found that out in The Salvation Army, if we had not done so before. Nevertheless, ours is not a religion of intellect, of culture, of refinement, of creeds, or of ceremony or forms. We attach very little importance to any of these in themselves. We gladly take hold of some of these, and use them as mediums through which to convey the living energy of the Spirit; but the *power is in the life,* not in the form. Where there is no life you can only get death. You may get it in beautiful forms, in beautiful ceremonies and symbols; but if there is no life you cannot beget life. The vital point is the life—the spirit. We have resuscitated this old-fashioned religion.

We defy infidels to account *on natural principles* for the results we have to show. We do not pretend that the presenting of certain truths to a man's intellect, even if he accepts those truths, will change his moral nature. We recognise the soul as the reigning power in man, and we

16

know that the only power that can really affect and transform the soul is the Spirit of God, therefore we do not attach much importance to people *merely receiving the truth!* Herein we differ very materially from most other evangelistic agencies.

I receive many letters from people after reading our books, congratulating us that we do not teach the Antinomian doctrines of a great deal of the evangelistic teaching of this day, that we don't preach the "only believe gospel," but that we preach repentance towards God, as well as faith in Jesus Christ, and a life of OBEDIENCE TO GOD, and that, without this, mere theories, creeds, and beliefs will only sink people lower into perdition. Our religion is not a religion of mere enjoyment, nor of faith only, but we recognise the power of God, transforming and keeping the soul of man.

Fourthly: *We are one in aim with the Churches.* Our object is the enlightenment and salvation and exaltation of the people. We have sacrificed all things for this. We have given, at any rate, the best proofs that human beings can give of our sincerity, in having made everything in our lives subservient to this one object. And surely this is the aim of all good and true men. Surely there is nobody professing to be the disciple of the Lord Jesus, who would say that their time, influence, position, and wealth ought to be consumed upon themselves! Surely men only actuated by philanthropy would say, "Of course these blessings must be used for the general good, for the exaltation and blessing of those who have not been so favoured by Providence."

A member of Parliament said, a short time ago, "If it were only for the material benefits you are conferring by the reformation of all these drunkards and blackguards, bringing them back to useful occupations and to the position of reliable citizens, you deserve well of your generation." We think so too; but then we think that this can only be permanently accomplished in one way. Here is where we differ from merely philanthropic and temporal reformers—the power of the Holy Ghost. We have had a great deal of experience, and we find that drunkards who sign the pledge, if they do not get the grace of God, soon fall back again. They want this spiritual restoration, and it is being actually accomplished on tens of thousands of them.

In conclusion, I think that these results ought to draw towards us the sympathy, prayer, and love of all really philanthropic, to say nothing of religious, men. If you think of this outlying continent of evil of which I have been speaking—millions of these untaught, uncivilized masses—if you just think that the Church, instead of *aggressing on this territory of the enemy,* is allowing that enemy to *aggress upon her!* what must be your conclusion? The churches of this land, it is admitted, are not keeping pace by a long way with the increase of the population, much less overtaking the lapsed multitudes beyond. Then you have only to keep going on at this rate, and you see what will happen! If vice continues to aggress upon virtue, you see what is before us as a nation. You have all the elements of demoralization, disorganization, and destruction existing in your midst today. They are only waiting the development of circumstances, and then look out! I am sure of that. The conviction is burnt into my very soul, and yet we cannot get the respectable and well-to-do classes to awaken to the fact.

"Oh!" as somebody said the other day, "the great want of this generation is public spirit." It is so difficult to get people to wake up to what is going on outside their own four walls. They separate themselves from these tumultuous elements and refuse to see them, and think themselves secure, when all the while they are sitting on the crater of a great volcano, which will, if they do not mind, burst and blow them up! What is to be done? Oh that God would awaken all really earnest and thoughtful men to ask this question! You must face this overwhelming torrent of evil with a direct antagonistic force of good, truth, righteousness, the fear and love of God, righteous living, and vigorous effort.

You can educate; but don't you know, some of you, the state of the educated classes? Is it any better than that of the uneducated? Has not the education only increased the capacity for mischief? You know it is so. You know how fast we have been going back for the last fifty years in morality. It was time somebody tried to do something; and we have tried, and God has owned and blessed our efforts. We have never allowed any consideration of interest, or ease, or aggrandisement, or popularity to weigh with us for one moment. We have been satisfied to know we have been doing the will of God. We have only waited to be satisfied in our own minds with respect to the steps we have taken, and then we have gone forward in the face of the world, and shall continue to do so. We want you to do so.

We do not say, "Do it in our way," only do it. Face the evil, and do something. Do not sit still in indifference and supineness. If you have any regard for your children, or for the future of this nation, or for the future destiny of the world, which so much hangs upon this nation, Do SOMETHING!

God only knows how deeply I desire that all godly men could present one common front to the foe, that we might be one in heart, one in purpose, and one in united effort. If this cannot be, let us all do our best. We intend to go on doing so, and we shall prepare the way for others. The Salvation Army is the friend of all and the enemy of none. We do not *hinder,* but *help* the churches. For whatever helps to humanize and civilize the people, must help the churches. If there is a little noise and *éclat* about our work, never mind. If the masses are better for it, as some writer has said, you must paint with a BIG BRUSH for the million, there will be room for you to operate when we have gone along.

As a rule, the churches have been revived and helped by our operations in most of the towns to which we have gone. It is one of the disadvantages under which we have laboured, that as our people get more refined and prosperous, many of them go off to the churches, leaving us to struggle on with the masses beneath; and these are the people who could most help us with funds. Therefore we feel we have a double claim upon the sympathy of Christians. As they get so much help from us, they ought to help us to roll the chariot on ahead and do the pioneering and scavenging. We have the testimony of many of the bishops and clergy and ministers of all denominations to the stirring up of zeal and effort in their churches attributable to the wide-spread influence of our movement; though, alas! on the whole, we get a poor return for it. I trust, however, that better things are to come.

3

The Founder and the Bishops

by Bramwell Booth

From *Echoes and Memories*, reprinted by Hodder and Stoughton, London, 1977. (originally published 1925).

AN interesting episode in the history of the Army was the series of discussions—or, shall I say, negotiations—which took place with certain distinguished leaders of the Church of England in the early eighties. The impulse to these negotiations really came out of the interest awakened in religious as well as irreligious circles by the rise and progress of the Army. Early in 1882 the then Archbishop of York (Dr. Thomson) wrote as follows to the Founder:

> Sir,—Some of my clergy have written to me to beg that I would ascertain how far it was possible for the Church to recognize the work of The Salvation Army as helping forward the cause of Christ consistently with our discipline. For this purpose they asked me to put myself into communication with your Leaders. I now, in compliance with their request, address you with this friendly object. ...
>
> Some of us think that you are able to reach cases, and to do so effectually, which we have great difficulty in touching. They believe that you are moved by zeal for God, and not by a spirit of rivalry with the Church, or any other agency for good, and they wish not to find themselves in needless antagonism with any in whom such principles and purposes prevail.

Shortly afterwards, the Lower House of Convocation petitioned the Upper House, that is, the House of Bishops, to issue some general instruction as to the attitude of the Church of England towards the Army. A committee was then appointed to consider the question, of which Dr. Benson, the Bishop of Truro, was the chairman. The instructions issued do not concern us here, but shortly after this the Founder received a letter from the Bishop in which, after referring to the growth of the work, he opened the subject of harmony with the Church. It was not purposed to enter upon any formal arrangements, but several of the bishops had desired to know more of the Movement and to make themselves acquainted with its spirit. If from a free interchange of views there should be found any way of cooperation with the Army many Christian people would rejoice. Would the General be willing to meet a few representatives of the Church for a friendly discussion? The Founder accepted this invitation.

The purpose which the Church of England authorities had in view was to find a means of linking up the Army in union with the Church. The principal ecclesiastics who took part in the negotiations were Dr. Benson, then Bishop of Truro, and afterwards Archbishop of Canterbury; Canon Westcott, of Westminster, and of the University of Cambridge—afterwards Bishop of Durham; Dr. Lightfoot, at that time Bishop of Durham; Canon Wilkinson, who was subsequently Bishop of Truro, and after that Bishop of St. Andrews; and Randall Davidson, the present Archbishop of Canterbury, who was then Dean of Windsor. With each of these I had some intercourse, and on one or two occasions met several of them together. Each one of them made a distinct impression upon me, which the passage of a long stretch of years has not effaced.

Dr. Davidson, the only one of the group who is now living, was acting in these negotiations as the representative of Dr. Tait, the then Archbishop of Canterbury. He struck me as a man who, while sincerely anxious to explore the ground and, if possible, to arrive at some means of linking The Salvation Army with his Church, and of helping forward its work, was yet fully determined, if this should be the issue, not to allow the Founder to continue in what was called his "autocratic" relationship. Evidently it was unthinkable to him that William Booth should ever become a high ecclesiastic in the Church of England, and for that reason alone he was careful to ensure that no power beyond what he could not help conceding should remain in the Founder's hands if the Army should come into alliance with his Church.

Dr. Davidson was very urbane and considerate throughout the negotiations, and although he was the rigid—not to say narrow—ecclesiastic, he showed real ability in fastening upon essentials when in conference with the Founder. I do not think he quite realized on his side how completely the Founder saw the "buttons on the back of his coat," but he did grasp the fact that he was not willing to relinquish his full control, no matter what advantages might be secured from the inclusion of himself and his Organization under the wing of the Church of England. So far as Dr. Davidson was concerned, this was, I am afraid, from the beginning, fatal to the project.

Canon Westcott's was quite a different type of church-manship. He was a scholar and recluse rather than a man experienced in ecclesiastical politics, and if a given end seemed to be desirable, he was inclined to underestimate any practical difficulties which might be in the way. I regarded him as one who really cared for the progress of religion, quite apart from the advancement either of the Church of England or of the Army. His influence upon the negotiations was that of a large-minded and sympathetic statesman, earnestly desirous of securing for his Church the accession of youthful zeal and vitality which unmistakably characterized the new Movement. He was, I dare say, more at home in the privacy of his study than at our round table, and he hardly realized how when a thing is theoretically desirable, its attainment may be impeded by obstructions which arise out of the nature of the case, and are not to be ascribed to the narrowness or obduracy of anybody. I carried away from our brief intercourse a deep impression of Dr. Westcott as a truly spiritual man; not exactly one of the old mystics, and yet possessed of a good deal of their vision and their charm. He was indeed a man to thank God for, no matter what age he lived in or to what Church he belonged.

Of Dr. Lightfoot I saw little; but here, again, the student and the scholar predominated. He was more willing than any of the others to leave the matter to Benson and Davidson. He spoke very kindly at that time in public, commending what he called the "apostolic zeal" of the Army. He remarked with great satisfaction that a large proportion of its converts and members were comparatively young people. To his thinking it was a grand testimony to the character of its message and to the efficacy of its work that this organization should be able to call to its banner the fiery and adventurous spirit of early manhood and womanhood. He also spoke with great appreciation of my dear mother's writings, and he joined heartily with Dr. Benson in desiring to bring about some kind of union with us.

Bishop Lightfoot's most memorable testimony to the work of the Army is found in his unforgettable words about the lost ideal of the work of the Church of Christ. Let the passage be quoted in full:

> Shall we be satisfied with going on as hitherto, picking up one here and one there, gathering together a more or less select congregation, forgetful meanwhile of the Master's command, 'Go ye into the highways and hedges, and compel them to come in'? The Salvation Army has taught us a higher lesson than this. Whatever may be its faults, it has at least recalled to us the lost ideal of the work of the Church, the universal compulsion of the souls of men.

Of the five negotiators perhaps I retain the happiest personal memory of Canon Wilkinson, afterwards Bishop of

Truro, and later of St. Andrews. Wilkinson was one of the sweetest men I ever knew, either within or without the Army borders. Both humble and sagacious, he had a gift for mediation and reconcilement which he had already put to good use in his own Church by intervening between the bishops and the ritualists. His feeling for the Army and some of its leaders was not simply admiration; it was love. He was the member of the group to take up the role of persuading the Founder to soften his conditions; and he it was who suggested with regard to the sacraments a compromise— which afterwards for a time bore some fruit—whereby the members of the Army were to be invited once a year to the Communion in their respective parish churches.

To the more strait-laced of the negotiators the accredited position which the women officers already occupied in the Army presented serious difficulty; and it was Wilkinson, again, who suggested that these comrades should be given an assured position and recognized as a body of dea-conesses, but that any future additions to their number should be required to go through a certain examination following our training. I think that Canon Wilkinson worked more arduously to bring about what they all desired than any of the others, and also that he had more faith than any of them for a practical outcome.

The Bishop of Truro, Dr. Benson, however, was the moving spirit in the negotiations. To him there had evidently come a kind of revelation of the new strength which the Church of England would acquire with the Army as its fighting auxiliary. His naturally sanguine temperament helped him to see not only what presented itself at the moment, but what was likely to come to pass in the future. He realized—and said as much—that the Army, which was then working in only three or four countries, was destined to play an awakening part in many lands. The Bishop of Minnesota (Dr. H. B. Whipple) had acquainted him with what the Army was beginning to do in the United States, and Benson saw an opportunity for that extension of the Church beyond the Old Land which his school of thought most earnestly desired.

I believe that Dr. Benson also had the best conception of the spiritual forces which the Army had released. Whereas the other negotiators, more particularly Dr. Davidson, centred their thought upon the leaders and their staff, Benson saw the Army *en masse.* Moreover, there was a prophetic vein in him. He had a vision of the future after the manner of Balaam, when he said of Israel of old, "from the top of the rocks I see him ... who can number the fourth part of Israel ... as the valleys are they spread forth, as trees which the Lord hath planted. ..."

Benson saw the Army as a force—a force which would go far and carry much; and subsequent events have abundantly proved that he was right. It was undoubtedly these considerations which stirred his spirit, and urged him to take the initiative. I never thought so highly of him intellectually as did some others who were more intimate with him. I cannot say that I regarded him as being of the calibre of Westcott or Lightfoot; but his combination of courtliness and candour, his genial freedom of manner and evident sincerity of feeling, made him lovable and unforgettable. There was something, half hidden, perhaps, but yet attractive, about his personal sympathy with heart religion, and therefore with our religion. He struck me, and I talked of it at the time, as a man who suddenly perceived in actual life what he had long looked for, more or less in vain. There, in flesh and blood, visible to all, were ordinary people who had renounced the pomp and glory of this world, who were really living for others, and who had organized the new-old conception of the Kingdom of God as for the *poor.* And, seeing it, he longed with a great longing to bring it into close union with himself and with the Church he loved.

All these men were, of course, Church of England men. They put the Church, to which they belonged, first in everything, and indeed nothing in our discussions involved the smallest departure on their part from a perfect loyalty to their own communion. But more than once we saw signs of the difficulties which undoubtedly confront all sincere thinkers when they come to claim, as the Church of England does claim, exclusive graces or privileges for any particular body of Christian people. The fact is, the Church of England is no more *the* Church than the Church at Jerusalem or the Church at Rome, or the Church of the Lutherans and Puritans, or the Church of the Calvinists and Presbyterians.

It was, of course, the purpose of our Lord Jesus Christ to gather out of the world a people composed of His true believing followers. This was spoken of in the New Testament as the Kingdom of Heaven or the Kingdom of God. It is obvious that in the accomplishment of this purpose a Body or Society would be formed distinct from the world in life, in purpose, and in interests, and that it would be generally recognized as such. This implies union and some form of organization, varying, no doubt, from time to time, but marked always under whatever form, by the possession of a certain common spirit—the spirit of Christ. "By their fruits ye shall know them." Thus we get a visible society—the society spoken of in the Bible as the Church or Congregation.[1] But as to the outward form which this society should take, Jesus Christ gave no recorded instruction. It is impossible to believe, if He had intended any particular constitution or form of government to be essential to this society—His Kingdom on earth—that He would not have left explicit directions with regard to it. Whereas on the whole matter He is entirely silent—says, in fact, nothing at all on the subject.

No, there is one Church. Just as there was only one people of Israel, no matter how widely scattered, so there is only one spiritual Israel. As Paul so finely says, "There is one body, and one Spirit, even as ye are called in one hope of

[1] In the original the same word stands for both.

27

your calling; one Lord; one faith, one baptism, one God and Father of all, who is above all, and through all, and in you all." And being one, yet it is to be for all people and all classes. In the Church of Christ "there is neither Greek nor Jew, circumcision nor uncircumcision, Barbarian, Scythian, bond nor free; but Christ is all and in all."

Of this, the Great Church of the Living God, we claim, and have ever claimed, that we of The Salvation Army are an integral part and element—a living fruit-bearing branch in the True Vine.

The idea that Jesus Christ in some way instituted a society with set orders of worship, and appointed the times and manner of sacred things, such as sacraments and sacrifices, or settled an order of ministers who should be the exclusive channel of grace, has no particle of authority in the New Testament. On the contrary, the fact is that He left His followers free to adopt such forms and methods, under the guidance and instruction from time to time of the Holy Spirit, as they should feel wisest and most appropriate to attain the objects in view. The Apostles did likewise, foreseeing that no matter how appropriate and wise might be the rules they could lay down for their day, other rules would be required for other times.

Dr. Lightfoot, to whom I have just been referring, expresses in his work on "The Christian Ministry" what is so entirely in harmony with our view on this point, that I shall quote him. He says:

The Kingdom of Christ, not being a kingdom of this world, is not limited by the restrictions which fetter other societies, political or religious. It is in the fullest sense free, comprehensive, universal. It displays this character not only in the acceptance of all comers who seek admission, irrespective of race or caste or sex, but also in the instruction and treatment of those who are already members. It has no sacred days or seasons, no special sanctuaries, because every time and every place alike are holy. Above all, it has no sacerdotal system. It interposes no sacrificial tribe or class between God and man by whose intervention God is reconciled and man forgiven. Each individual member holds personal communion with the Divine

28

*Head. To Him immediately he is responsible, and from Him directly
he obtains pardon and draws strength.*

Further, as to the calling out and setting apart of leaders in
the days of early Christianity, we find also a wonderful record
of freedom and a remarkable likeness to what happened with
us. No one who knows the Army can study the story of our
Lord's selecting and calling the Twelve without being struck
by the similarity in many respects—I say this with all
reverence—of our method with His. And the glimpses of
further calls which we get in the Acts illustrate also our
nearness to Apostolic plans. The early Christian leaders—
that is of the first hundred years—proceeded much as we
have done. They dealt with a not dissimilar kind of material,
chiefly uneducated and poor working people—and, guided
by the Spirit of God, they adopted means for spreading and
establishing the work just as the Founder and those who
gathered around him, also led by the Spirit of God, adopted
means, and not dissimilar means, for us—means which we
still follow.

On this subject it is of interest to read the earliest Christian
writing (apart from the New Testament) which now remains
in the world—a letter from a celebrated man of that time
whose life in part ran parallel with the concluding years of the
lives of many of the first Apostles. Clement of Rome, in about
the year A.D. 96-8, says:

> *The Apostles received the Gospel for us from the Lord Jesus
> Christ; Jesus Christ was sent forth from God. Christ then was from
> God, and the Apostles from Christ. Both therefore were from the will
> of God in perfect order. Having then received commands, and being
> fully assured through the resurrection of our Lord Jesus Christ, and
> being confirmed in the word of God with full assurance of the Holy
> Ghost, they went forth, preaching the good tidings that the Kingdom
> of God was at hand. Preaching therefore from country to country,
> and from city to city, they appointed their first fruits [that is the
> converts], having tested them by the Spirit, to be bishops and
> deacons to them that should believe.[2]*

[2] It will be noted that no reference is here made to "ordination," but to
appointing; nor to "sacraments," but to the good tidings.

29

The word rendered "bishop" means literally *overseer,* and would answer to our divisional officer—one who came to have the oversight of several of the congregations or societies of Christian disciples. The word "deacon" means minister or servant. The "deacon" was the first visiting official, he cared for the sick, and distributed the alms of the society among the poor as well as gave instruction in the Scripture. The deacon of those early days answers in many matters to the field officer of our own early history.

We believe then that our Lord Jesus Christ has called us into His Church of the Redeemed, that our call has not been by man or the will of man, but by the Holy Spirit of God; that our salvation is from Him, not by ceremonies or sacraments or ordinances of this period or of that, but by the pardoning life-giving work of our Divine Saviour. We believe also that our system for extending the knowledge and power of His Gospel, and of nurturing and governing the believing people gathered into our ranks, is as truly and fully in harmony with the spirit set forth and the principles laid down by Jesus Christ and His Apostles as those which have been adopted by our brethren of other times or of other folds.

In this we humbly but firmly claim that we are in no way inferior, either to the saints who have gone before, or— though remaining separate from them, even as one branch in the Vine is separate from another—to the saints of the present. We, no less than they, are called and chosen to sanctification of the Spirit and to the inheritance of eternal life. And our officers are, equally with them, ministers in the Church of God, having received diversities of gifts, but the one Spirit—endowed by His Grace, assured of His guidance, confirmed by His Word, and commissioned by the Holy Ghost to represent Him to the whole world. Speaking of this matter in 1894, the Founder said:

> *The Salvation Army is not inferior in spiritual character to any Christian organization in existence. We are in no wise dependent on the Church....If it perished off the face of the earth to-morrow we*

should be just as efficient for the discharge of the duties we owe to men as we are to-day. ... We are, I consider, equal every way and everywhere to any other Christian organization on the face of the earth (i) in spiritual authority, (ii) in spiritual intelligence, (iii) in spiritual functions. We hold "the keys" as truly as any Church in existence.

But I must return to the bishops. In the course of the negotiations Benson and Davidson visited, either by appointment or quite unknown, certain Salvation Army centres, and were present at typical meetings. Of his visits Dr. Davidson afterwards wrote:

Whatever be their errors in doctrine or in practice, I can only say that, after attending a large number of meetings of different kinds in various parts of London, I thank God from my heart that He has raised up to proclaim His message of salvation the men and women who are now guiding the Army's work, and whose power of appealing to the hearts of their hearers is a gift from the Lord Himself. I am sorry for the Christian teacher, be he cleric or layman, who has listened to such addresses as those given by General Booth, Mrs. Booth, and by some five or six at least of their "staff officers," who has not asked help that he may speak his message with the like straightforward ability and earnest zeal.

Among the places to which Dr. Benson came was the Training Garrison at Clapton. His purpose was to look over the buildings, see something of the character of the students and of their work, and from this to form a judgment. He was late for his appointment that morning, and by the time he arrived I was conducting one of our ordinary prayer meetings with officers. As soon as he learned that this was in progress he sent word that he would like presently to come into the service, where he hoped I would allow him to remain for at least a part of the time. Accordingly while I went on with the meeting, he looked round the buildings, saw something of the cadets, the classes and text-books and at last came into the lecture hall. He entered at the back, and, apart from myself, no one was aware of his presence. Some two hundred officers were on their knees, and the meeting was one of liberty and fervour, with hearty responses and moving singing. We were having what we call a "good time."

After watching the meeting, on his knees, for nearly an hour, the Bishop, seeing that it was about to conclude, withdrew, and waited for me in one of the reception rooms. I was a little doubtful of the kind of impression such a gathering would have made upon him, not in any degree because I questioned its naturalness or rightness, but because its extreme freedom and its noise were in such contrast to the modes of worship to which he was accustomed. As I came into the room he rose from his seat, took both my hands in his, and before I could say a word, exclaimed, "O, my dear brother, the Holy Spirit is with you!" I began to explain certain of the incidents which it might have been difficult for him to appreciate, but he stopped me, remarked on the evident *sincerity* of it all, and gave me Godspeed.

There the story tails off. It is left with a rather ragged edge. Tait died, Benson became Archbishop of Canterbury, and Wilkinson Bishop of Truro. Other topics filled the mind, and other duties became urgent. My feeling is that the Founder unquestionably adopted the right course in these negotiations. I never took upon myself, nor did Railton, who was now in our inner councils, to urge upon the Founder that the freedom for which he had paid so great a price should in no case be forfeited, if its forfeiture meant the furtherance of what we all had more deeply at heart. We were aware that some kind of union with the Church of England would enhance our position in the eyes of the public, and that it would not only clear our financial skies in the immediate present, but probably enormously increase our resources for the future.

But just as Dr. Davidson felt that the question of authority was the real difficulty, so we saw on our side that the absence of authority was a grave weakness of the Church of England, and that its sacrifice on our part would involve the ruin of the Army. There was nothing little or petty in this. It was not a point of personal prestige or dignity; it was simply that the so-called "autocracy," although it might lay us open to misunderstanding, was necessary for the effectiveness of our war. Railton here was a wise counsellor. He had already seen the Army beginnings in other lands; he foresaw it encircling the globe, and he felt—as we all came to feel— that to barter the very thing which made the Army capable of such prompt mobility and such singleness of front could only prove disastrous.

We must admit that had it been possible to reach some kind of combination, or even a treaty of mutual support, The Salvation Army would have been greatly helped, and there would have been an infusion of new enthusiasm and energy and spiritual life into the Church of England. Part of the energy and devotion which have been turned into High Church channels would have been guided into spheres of activity much more fruitful to the Church and useful to the world, and as I firmly believe, much more honouring to God. But it was not to be. And yet the Army is marching on!

4

The Man Whom the Churches Excommunicated

by Rev. Principal Thomas Phillips, D.D.
President - National Free Church Council. An
address delivered at centenary of the Founder's
birth, London, April 10, 1929.

From *The Staff Review,* May 1929, published
by The Salvation Army, International Headquarters, London.

THE Prime Minister has spoken for the West Midlands and
said it was a most important part of the British Empire.
There is another part of the British Empire called Wales, and
Wales is proud to have a representative on the platform this
evening.

I am perfectly at home in representing Cardiff and Wales. I
am not quite so much at home in representing the Free
Churches; for William Booth started as a Free Churchman
but he did not do much until he had got rid of us and we got
rid of him! It was when the Free Churches excommunicated
him that God began to use him! The Free Churches were not
big enough.

Hence we are face to face with this tremendous fact: That
at a time when organized Christianity was thought to be
essential, perhaps the greatest work for God was done
outside the Christian Church, by a Christian man whom the
Christian Church excommunicated!

No wonder we did not know what to make of him. When I
was in America about six months ago I read a poem, for

which I have been looking all day. It described the consternation in Heaven occasioned by the arrival of William Booth waving the flag of the Army, and beating the drum, so the angels did not know what to do. And if the angels could not understand him how could you expect the Free Churches to understand him? At any rate, *he did his work clean outside the Church!*

Of the way the churches of the country, including the Free Churches, often spend their days and nights talking of ordination and Church order, William Booth knew nothing. He was never ordained—he was too busy holding meetings—he had no ordination meeting. But in reading his life story written by Harold Begbie I found he was ordained—ordained by a woman—ordained by one of the most saintly women of the century, by his wife, Catherine Booth. There was a great Free Church meeting, a great conference, and the question discussed was: would William Booth toe the line? Would he consent to give up his enthusiasm and just be a decent, respectable parson? And William Booth grunted, as his leaders pressed and his friends persuaded, and did not know what to do. Then he looked up to the gallery, to a woman there who did not belong to the conference, and she stood up and said, "William, never!" And William took up his overcoat and walked out of the Free Churches for ever. That is how a woman ordained William Booth outside organized Christianity!

But there is something more serious than that! We orthodox churches believe in sacraments, in baptism—I am a Baptist—and in communion. And yet here comes along this man and *he has no use for them at all!* And all the sacraments go, and a great Church is built up in this modern land of ours without any emphasizing of sacraments, and the kingdom of God goes on growing independently of sacraments!

But, mind, *you Salvationists have a spiritual equivalent of the sacraments.* For baptism you have a *Penitent-Form.* The best baptismal service I ever attended was at a Salvation Army meeting on the Thames Embankment, in company with Staff-Captain McGregor. I preached in one of your pulpits at two o'clock one morning to a number of tramps, and if I ever preached the Gospel I preached it then. At the end, I asked, "Will any man confess the Lord Jesus Christ?" and a sturdy, athletic tramp stood up and said, *"I do!"* The rest jeered at the man, and he turned and said, "You can laugh at me, but I am prepared to fight any man in the place!" He confessed and was prepared to defend his faith. If that is not the spirit of baptism I do not know what is!

And for the communion service you have the *Knee-Drill.*

This man rejected the sacraments in such a way that no Christian Church in the whole British Empire but one—the Quakers—would admit him to Church membership! And yet, all the churches are here to-night to honour this man! This man got hold of *the spirit* of the sacraments but dispensed with *the forms* of them.

Then there was another thing: He did not treat the devil with the same respect as the churches do. We, as churches, are very timid of the devil. We like to keep the devil at a respectable distance. We believe in fortifications—great churches, great services, great preachers; we are inclined as churches to dig ourselves into trenches. William Booth was "over the top" every time! He preferred to be out in the open with the devil.

Take three illustrations: First of all, musical hall songs. We, as churches, said, "Oh, do not disturb the beauty, the dignity of our service by questionable music." But when the devil got a decent music hall song, William Booth stole it and had it at The Salvation Army citadel! I do not think anyone ever treated the devil so unfairly—he captured all his best points. We, as representing the Free Churches, like to *smash* the devil's guns, but William Booth *captured* them and *used* them, and did a good deal of shooting with the devil's guns.

Take another example: money. William Booth saw brewers

had a lot of money, and said, "Why should brewers have God's money? The money is used for making beer. Why shouldn't it be annexed—any money, no matter from whom—it has been used long enough in the devil's business. Let us put it to God's business."

And yet more important than these, he captured the devil's biggest gun, and that is *the fighting spirit.* This militarism, he said, is in us all. All of us will fight on *bad* lines if we are not set fighting on *good* lines; this fighting spirit, instead of being used for killing bodies, should be captured for The Salvation Army and turned to saving souls. That was a magnificent stroke of genius—indeed, one of the greatest strokes of his genius.

William James, the great American philosopher, made quite a stir by his essay on what he termed "the moral equivalent of war," but William Booth, over thirty years before, by his spiritual equivalent of war so captured the devil's guns as to use them to win the battles of the Lord.

It is amazing how this man took hold of our cherished convictions and made mincemeat of them! There is a story in the life of Abraham Lincoln to the effect that General Grant and his army reached a river and had to cross it. Grant turned to his architect and said, "We want a bridge." While the architect went to his tent to draw a sketch of a bridge, an old rough army carpenter went down to the river, and, helped by a few practical men, quickly put up a bridge. He then went back to the General and said, "Them pictures ain't come yet, but the bridge is up!" That is it exactly. While we are trying to settle our theology and to settle our *Churchanity*—and they need some settling—and to settle our differences about the sacraments; while we are busy with our philosophies and theological differences, while we are all busy in our tents painting our pictures, William Booth and you go down to the river, and the bridge is put up!

5

The Salvation Army in its Relation to the Churches

by Maud Ballington Booth

From *Beneath two Flags*. Published by Funk and Wagnalls, New York, 1889.

*Enough and too much of the sect and
   the name
What matters our label, so truth be our
   aim?
The creed may be strange, but the life
   may be true,
And hearts beat the same under drab
   coats or blue.*

- Whittier

* * *

*The existing forms may disappear, but
the truth, the soul of religion will
revive more vigorous than ever.*

- A.J. Froude

THERE is perhaps no question which needs more thoroughly to be understood and appreciated than the Army's relation to the many Christian denominations who are fighting in different parts of the battlefield, but yet beneath the banner of the Cross; and there is no doubt that a very wrong and harmful impression has been created by those who have not understood the movement to the effect that Salvationists are directly antagonistic, or, at least far from friendly toward other Christian bodies.

This erroneous idea might possibly arise from the fact that our measures and *modus operandi* are so entirely different from the forms already existing in other Christian bodies. It is quite true that the Army services are conducted very differently from those of other Christians. We do not build fine edifices with spires and steeples, chimes of bells, and other embellishments... If in these things we followed the customs and traditions of the churches we should be utterly defeated in the special work which the Army has undertaken. There are sects and denominations enough. This is an Army, a band of aggressive men and women warriors, whose work of saving and reclaiming the world must be done on entirely new lines to obtain the results, without which they would not dare to consider their work a success. These denominations have tried and have repeatedly confessed that they have failed in gaining the desired result, which has very often been not from want of good intentions, but from inefficacy of measures.

Talking of ordinary religious methods, as compared with those of The Salvation Army, Walsham Howe, the late Bishop of Bedford, said: "Why, what do these poor souls (the drunken masses) know of all this? You might as well talk Greek to them as tell them much of what I have told you. Talk of heavenly affections and love of holiness to men wallowing in the filth of the foulest lusts! Talk of the blessedness of a life of prayer to men who use God's name only for curses! Talk of the power and grace of sacrifices to men who have no conception of anything beyond what their senses tell them! Talk of the grand old creeds to men who have never realized the very first words, 'I believe in God!' Talk of unselfishness to men who have never acted on any other motive than self! Talk of happiness in religion to men whose only idea of happiness is the indulgence of the passing passions! Oh, my friends, there is something to do before all this. We want to tell these poor souls just the very first and simplest things. We have got to tell them as we would our own little children, of a God who loves them, of a Saviour who died for them that they might live, of a Spirit who will help them to break their fetters and be free."

Again, it is very possible that the fiery zeal, the aggressive spirit, and marked success that are visible in our corps might be taken as reflections upon some quiet, slow-going churches; but the fact that the Army example in that way is condemnatory to others can no more be blameworthy in them than it was in Jesus Christ, when, by His loving zeal for the salvation of publicans and sinners, He brought out in striking contrast the hypocritical lives of Pharisees, whose prayer and religious ordinances proved but a whited sepulchre to their worldly, unbelieving hearts. But the Army's working thus seeming to reflect upon dead and inconsistent parts of the Christian world should only stimulate and encourage the good and devoted of every denomination.

It can hardly be disputed that the Christian churches of the present day are far from what they ought to be. Taking Christ's standard of religion, the zeal for sinners, the seeking of the poor who are moneyless and positionless, the imitating and following of the despised Man of Sorrows, have, to the bitter regret and sorrow of all true-hearted Christians, been acknowledged to be very much lacking in the hearts of many who call themselves by the name of Christ. The Salvation Army, of course, cannot be blind to these facts, but they recognize it as one of the most important principles of their Christian warfare to let charity "abound unto all men," and it is a stringent rule that no Salvation Army officer is allowed to speak against or run down any church or Christian work, but to stand upon a footing of brotherly friendship with every true and sincere follower of Christ. There are faults and flaws undoubtedly that could be picked in some

41

Salvation Army corps, for the organization is as yet struggling and striving for greater perfection; and knowing that there may be some panes of glass in their own house, they would be the last to turn upon others and throw stones. Should anything be said from Salvation Army platforms or in Salvation Army publications regarding the coldness or worldliness or bitterness which can be found in the Christian world of the present day, let it be thoroughly and forever understood that such words would only be uttered generally and in condemnation of false and Christless Christians and as a warning to others; but in no way personally to any church or with the intention of hurting or discouraging the good, true, and earnest who are striving to do the work which God has allotted to them to the utmost of their ability, though possibly in a very different way from The Salvation Army.

I am sorry to say that this rule has not always been adhered to by our critics, who, we can but wish in some instances, had more Christian love toward us and regard for themselves than to publicly and violently denounce us.

We expected bitter opposition to the death from saloonkeepers, infidels, worldlings, and God-haters in general, but I am sorry to have to chronicle the fact that many of the most bitter attacks against The Salvation Army have been hurled from the pulpits or written by the pens of Christians; and it is but natural to feel that it would have been a far more Christian thing if we were thought in the wrong to have come and told us so personally, so that any such wrong could be set right; or to have prayed to the God whom we serve in common that He might guide us out of error into truth. But when such attacks have been made with evident spleen in public, not to an audience of Salvationists, but poured into the ears of godless, unsympathetic listeners, it has been very apparent that the motive was not one of loving advice or remonstrance, but was prompted by an uncharitable spirit, unless, as we have often tried to believe, it was through misunderstanding or a scanty knowledge, which had proved insufficient to the forming of a correct judgment.

But even should it be thus, it is surprising that men of education should feel it necessary to speak in condemnation of any movement of whose methods and principles and successes they had not made a careful study. Through all this the Army maintains its principle of non-interference with other Christians; for, indeed, we believe that the schisms and bickerings and enmities which have, since the Christian era, cropped up in the Church are far more damaging to the cause of Christ than any outside opposition from un-believers, and therefore we have tried, as far as in us lieth, "to live peaceably with all men."

Of course, some individual soldier or officer in this great organization might break through this rule, or some outsider not under our control might speak in a meeting, and inveigh against some creed or doctrine or religion to which they were opposed; but were it known to the leaders of the Army, it would be instantly condemned, being thoroughly contrary to the doctrines and disciplines.

As we are antagonistic to no special sect, and strive to carry out Jesus Christ's spirit in the treatment of all kinds and conditions of men as one, whether they be Jews or Gentiles, rich or poor, the Army has become known as the friend of all and the teacher and propagator of no new division in the Christian world, but a rallying point for many of the zealous in every branch of God's work and the raiser of the lost.

As has been explained in a previous chapter, The Salvation Army having in one sense not been a man-made organization, nor evolving from the brain of its leader, but having been wonderfully and strangely led by God from plan to plan, step by step, the former ideas of the General, as years advanced, had to be laid aside, and instead of sending his converts into the different churches and conducting his work simply on revival plans, it became absolutely neces-

43

sary to gather his converts together round the flag and form an Army.

One of the special reasons why his first plan of drafting them off into the churches proved impracticable, was the fact that these young converts, so many of them brought from the very depths of sin, needed to be thoroughly and wholly occupied in God's service; for had they been left without work, the first love and warmth of large numbers would have faded away, and they would have ceased to be any spiritual good to God or man; and it was found in many of the then existing churches that there was a lack in young members and converts not having any such work, hence having to stand idly by without any active employment in God's service. All effort so often has wrongly ceased at the point of conversion, as if that was the ultimatum and end of work, instead of being the real beginning and first step in the Christian life—and with the class with which the Army especially deals this would have been ruinous in the extreme; thus the Army has proved valuable with its methods, which can employ every convert, from the youngest to the oldest, in responsible and active work.

It should be clearly understood, however, that this organization can in no way be regarded as wishing to steal and use those who are already church-members. So much are we opposed to this that even when men and women have been converted in Army meetings, who have come from constant attendance at churches, they have been told to go back and spread the fire in their own church. The Army has wished to recruit and keep in its ranks only those who formerly belonged to no particular denomination.

Of course, this cannot always be done, as there have been some who have persistently refused to return to their churches, feeling that God has called them into the Army work, and they can work there as nowhere else for His glory; but, on the other hand, tens of thousands saved or sanctified while in Army meetings have returned to their churches, carrying the fire, zeal, and love thus gained back to their own people, to help in that sphere to spread the Christian work which before they cared but little about. It is a perfectly erroneous idea to think that The Salvation Army invites or induces or even advises the members of any church to leave their own and enter its ranks, though, on the other hand, many of our people have been taken from us and appropriated by different churches, going greatly to augment their numbers and their zeal.

Last winter in a New England city a certain church had a revival, while among the most active workers were a score of young men and women who were frequenters of Army meetings, several of them having lately been at the Army penitent-form seeking the blessing of a clean heart. In the midst of the revival, the pastor, while giving some general instructions, urged them to attend only their own church, and thereby "not spread the fire." This was so evidently aimed at the Army, that a venerable church member, a true friend of Salvationists, could not let it pass, and told him that they attended Army meetings "not to *spread* the fire, but to *get* it."

Not only is this the Army's attitude toward the churches, but taking its work from another point of view, it can be easily proved that it has been a real benefit to them instead of a hindrance. In almost any town where The Salvation Army has been working for six months or so, it has stirred up fresh interest in religious matters, and it will be found that not only do they gather together large crowds, but the attendance at the churches is greatly increased also, and that the general interest revived in religion can be made of great use and help to any minister who will avail himself of it.

Unquestionably, another advantage that the Army has proved to the churches has been the showing to them the awful need of revival of aggressive work and extraordinary effort to reach the careless, Godless, hitherto unreachable masses.

The Bishop of Durham says on this point: "Shall we be

satisfied with going on as hitherto, picking up one here and one there, gathering together a mere select congregation, forgetful meanwhile of the Master's command, 'Go out into the highways and hedges and compel them to come in'? The Salvation Army has taught us a higher lesson than this. Whatever may be its faults, it has at least recalled us to this lost ideal of the work of the Church, the universal compulsion of the souls of men."

The Archbishop of York writes: "Even the wild march of The Salvation Army stirs the Church up to recognize her duty, and we would do well to learn many valuable lessons from these holy enthusiasts."

Then it has also shown an example of devotion and zeal. Church-members, from their comfortable pews watching the toil, poverty, and self-sacrificing spirit of devoted Army officers, have felt ashamed of their own sitting at ease in Zion, and have gone forth into God's vineyard—some as missionaries, some into the ministry, and some to stand by the minister's side and make perfect revolutions in the revival line in their own churches. Many and many a time have we heard from the lips of those whose profession of Christianity benefited only themselves, and not God's lost ones out in the desert, expressions of regret and shame for their want of zeal and love and interest—a confession which has often been followed by a determined seeking for the power, grace, and love which have revolutionized their lives and enabled them to revolutionize the lives of others.

Again, the very methods that have been adopted by The Salvation Army, though at first much criticised and ridiculed, have in time been initiated or adopted by those who were desirous of reaching the classes who they had found by experience could not be reached by the means they had hitherto employed. Oh, what consternation was manifested at a band of Christian workers being called The Salvation Army! What objections and what criticisms as to the military terms, the banners, the street parades, and the using of converts in the place of educated speakers! But since that time all these things have most surely been endorsed and accepted as useful by many different churches, for a great many different Armies have sprung up during the last ten years.

The Church of England has its Church Army; the Methodists have an Army and a paper like our *War Cry,* called the *Battle Axe;* then there is the Blue Ribbon Army, the White Ribbon Army, and the Gospel Army; and even those who do not call themselves Armies are still adopting many of the measures employed by our organization. Salvation Army hymns, both words and music, can be found in almost all the revival hymn-books of the present day, though at one time the lively, rousing song-tunes employed by us were considered thoroughly out of place and decorum. Surely these things should go to show the Christian public that even people who do not publicly sympathize with us thus positively endorse our methods by copying them.

Many of the world's pulpits are at the present day being faithfully filled by men converted in The Salvation Army. Several hundreds of those converted under Mrs. General Booth's administration alone have gone out to engage in public Christian service, and a large number of those already in the ministry have been sanctified and blessed at our holinesss meetings, which are one of the strongest points of The Salvation Army, and one of the principles in which it has most helped and taught churches. Here is the written testimony of an Episcopal clergyman upon the subject:

"What has The Salvation Army done for me? It opened my eyes, took me by the hand and led me into the kingdom of God. After a ministry of seventeen years, I learned first in The Salvation Army, six years ago, to know Jesus Christ as my personal Saviour in a way I had never known Him before.

"Through The Salvation Army, as God's chosen instrument, I passed out of an Egyptian bondage of narrow

47

ecclesiasticism into the glorious liberty of the children of God, no longer a servant but a son.

"From a dry and wooden traditionalism—teaching for doctrines the commandments of men—I passed through the simple teaching of the Army into the fresh, lifegiving teaching of the Holy Ghost Himself—from preaching *about* Christ to preaching Christ and Him only.

"For years I had believed in and taught the need of conversion. In The Salvation Army, for the first time, I saw men and women converted on the spot—entering the room lost and helpless wrecks in body and soul, leaving the meeting saved and rejoicing in God.

"I had always believed in the Holy Ghost as the Lord and Life-giver. In the meetings of The Salvation Army I first realized in my own soul, and saw realized in others the baptism of the Spirit and what is meant by Heaven opening and the Spirit of God descending like a dove and lighting upon the heart, and filling soul and body with a very heaven of joy and peace.

"In one night of prayer, never to be forgotten, I left behind me forever the fear of man and passed into the love and life of God in Christ Jesus.

"From that hour the blessing has grown and deepened with my life, and for these past six years that life has been one sweet song of praise, a strong hallelujah of soul, glad news, which my lips can but feebly express in words.

"The past six years have been by far the richest and happiest of the whole twenty-three since I was ordained, and every hour I live gives proof of the reality and depth of the mighty change wrought in me by God through The Salvation Army.

"May God bless it and all its noble workers more than ever, and make it to many a brother minister what it has certainly been to me—the *greatest spiritual blessing of my life.*"

—Henry Wilson.

Another minister wrote me a few months ago as follows: "I praise the Lord that through you He gave me so much of that 'greater power' which I longed for and which we prayed for, as seen in our services of yesterday. Last night my inquiry room was well filled, and the blessed Jesus sanctified the Word. It does me so much good to write you this, and it may cheer your heart to know of it, for I am myself one of your reconsecrated children. When you addressed your audience in Association Hall on the success of your work, you seemed to take a satisfaction in saying that the Army had been the instrument in blessing ministers. The next time you speak and make the statement, you may have the assurance that one more, and that another New York clergyman, received richly of God's grace through the same instrumentality. My whole soul blesses His Holy Name. May He and the Lord Jesus continue to uphold you and your workers in His cause."

The following testimonies are from well-known ministers of different denominations, who, having watched The Salvation Army, have a right to judge of it.

The Rev. Asbury Lowrey, D.D., says: "To say that all the methods of The Salvation Army are according to my taste, would be to utter an untruth; but when I see the absolute need of the adoption of some effectual measures to arrest the attention of the countless multitudes who throng the way of death, I fling my little objection to the winds, under the conviction that the salvation of these perishing masses is not a question of taste, but a question of necessity and haste. It may be a very distasteful truth, but still it remains a truth, that the churches signally fail to reach the lower strata of society and but few of the upper classes. We are standing face to face with the dismal and crushing fact that the churches are a failure so far as reaching the great bulk of sinners is concerned.

"Just how much good has been done by The Salvation

Army it is impossible to estimate; but one fact is reduced to history, that this unique agency has been a new epoch in the methods of reaching the lower and most neglected classes."

Mr. Spurgeon says: "If The Salvation Army were wiped out of London, five thousand extra policemen could not fill its place in the repression of crime and disorder."

Dr. McMurdy says: "The religious world is professedly pacific. The labor world is professedly converted to arbitration and peace. Let us advance a step further and enlist the fighting element to contend for peace, bringing the whole community into martial trim for heroic, enthusiastic demonstrations, and for final victory over the tyrant War.

"We have an agency in the thousands of drilled soldiers of The Salvation Army in America, and their millions scattered over all lands, which is a missionary against war, as against rum, tobacco, and dissipation."

Dr. Talmage said, recently: "It makes but little difference whether the world and the Church like or dislike The Salvation Army. It is evident that the Lord approves it. Witness the multitudes of its converts—the sinful reclaimed, the degraded elevated, the drunkard reformed, and the ever-widening influence for good plainly seen by all those whose eyes have not been closed by bigotry, prejudice, and sin. The combined forces of earth and hell cannot hinder this evangelical movement."

The Rev. Mr. Goss, of Chicago, says: "I say The Salvation Army is good. I believe it to be a heaven-born organization, for there is a stratum of human life which none but these people are reaching—a stratum which men and women who live in cultured homes should not forget. Jesus Christ looks down weeping upon them. If there is any one who has been out of sympathy with this movement, go home, think about it, pray about it, remember that if a man has a foul cellar, a pestilence-breeding cellar under his dwelling, he should be thankful to any one who would go down and clean it out, no matter how it was done, as long as he reaped the benefit of it.

This is what The Salvation Army is doing for us."

The Salvation Army does not court the praise or favor of any man, be he Christian or not; but sympathy and encouragement such as we have just quoted can but be cheering in so arduous a war as ours, and we can but feel that it is only a matter of time ere the good and earnest in every church, as they learn to know the Army, will stretch out to it the hand of fellowship.

> *Is not a day coming—yes, unto them who watch for the morning has it not already dawned?—when we shall grow so covetous of good and grace as to turn our swords, too often sharpened against each other's bosoms, into ploughshares, to break up the fallow ground that lies within us and around us—when we shall beat our spears into pruning-hooks to dress the abundant increase of the days—when the sower shall overtake the reaper, and the treader of grapes him that soweth seed?—D. E. Greenwell.*

6

The Nature of the Church

by Frederick Coutts

From *The Salvation Army in Relation to the Church,* The Salvation Army, International Headquarters, London, 1978.

THE place of The Salvation Army within the Christian community known (among other titles) as "the Body of Christ" (I Corinthians 12:17), "the Bride of Christ" (2 Corinthians 11:2), "the household of faith" (Galatians 6:10), "the Israel of God" (Galatians 6:16), and "the people of God" (1 Peter 2:10)—all New Testament descriptions of "that company of people who acknowledge Jesus as God and Saviour, and in whose midst the Holy Spirit is manifest"—has long been an area of sensitive concern both to those without as well as within the Movement itself.

This could have been why, early in 1882, the Lower House of Convocation of the Church of England petitioned the Upper House for guidance as to what should be their attitude towards the Army. The upshot was that in May of the same year the bishops of the Canterbury Convocation appointed a committee "to consider how far the Army could be attached to the Church of England"[1]—on which inquiry the Arch-

[1] Owen Chadwick, *The Victorian Church* (A. & C. Black), Pt. II, p. 205.

bishop of Canterbury was represented by E. W. Benson, at that time Bishop of Truro. Nor were the Army leaders of that day unaware that "some kind of union with the Church of England would enhance our position in the eyes of the public, and ... not only clear our financial skies in the immediate present, but probably enormously increase our resources for the future."[2]

The ensuing conversations were marked by cordiality on both sides. J. B. Lightfoot, Bishop of Durham, spoke of the way in which the Army had "recalled to us the lost ideal of the work of the Church, the universal compulsion of the souls of men." Canon Westcott deeply impressed Bramwell Booth as "a truly spiritual man ... a man to thank God for." Randall Davidson, then Dean of Windsor, wrote: "I thank God from my heart that He has raised up to proclaim His message of salvation the men and women who are now guiding the Army's work."

Nevertheless, the final results were inconclusive, even though William Booth was prepared to acknowledge the Church of England by arranging for Army corps to attend divine worship at the local parish church at agreed inter- vals—and this in full uniform.[3] But the committee appointed by the bishops did not even report back and, to be fair, William Booth allowed the negotiations to lapse as well. The story was left with "a rather ragged edge," was Bramwell Booth's verdict. "Opinion swung so unfavourably against the Army," Owen Chadwick has written, "that the old talk of 'attachment' to the church looked wild." The cause of this is nowhere stated in *The Victorian Church,* but in the following year public—though unproven—charges of condoning im- morality were made against the Army, and two years later Bramwell Booth was personally involved in the crusade to raise the age of consent.[4]

[2] Bramwell Booth, *Echoes and Memories* (Hodder & Stoughton, paperback), p. 84.

[3] Harold Begbie, *William Booth* (Macmillan), II, p. 34ff.

[4] *Bread for my Neighbor* (Hodder & Stoughton, paperback), p. 45ff.

Meanwhile, Catherine Booth had been giving a series of public addresses in London—printed under the title of *The Salvation Army in Relation to the Church and State*—making it clear that this new and (to some) unpleasantly vigorous Movement had no quarrel with the existing churches, nor with their policy, nor with their theology. "When their doctrines were examined," commented Chadwick, "the Salvationists were found to teach two very simple truths also taught by the Church of England—those of sin and redemption."[5] Mrs. Booth was but spelling out her husband's remark to the Archbishop of Canterbury that "we do not seek to justify our own existence by finding fault with yours."

Nevertheless, there was undeniably "a ragged edge"—if only because those involved in these conversations shared no agreed definition of the Church as such. This is not to say that those who represented the Primate had no such definition. They had—and so had William Booth. "We believe," wrote his eldest son, "that our system for extending the knowledge and power of His gospel, and of nurturing and governing the believing people gathered into our ranks, is as truly and fully in harmony with the spirit set forth and the principles laid down by Jesus Christ and His apostles as those which have been adopted by our brethren of other times or other folds.

"In this, we humbly but firmly claim that we are in no way inferior, either to the saints who have gone before, or—though remaining separate from them, even as one branch in the Vine is separate from another—to the saints of the present. We, no less than they, are called and chosen to sanctification of the Spirit and to the inheritance of eternal life. And our officers are, equally with them, ministers in the Church of God, having received diversities of gifts, but the one Spirit. ..."[6]

It should be remembered that when, on July 18, 1861,

[5] Chadwick, p. 295

[6] Bramwell Booth, p. 82.

William Booth left his assured place as a Superintendent Minister in the Methodist New Connexion, he did not think of himself as leaving the Church. "I offer myself," he wrote even in his letter of resignation, "for the evangelistic work, in the first instance to our own connexional churches, and, when they decline to engage me, to other portions of the religious community."[7]

This was not the language of a man who was washing his hands of the Church, but of one who could only be faulted for his great eagerness that the mission of the Church might be fulfilled more effectively. To remind ourselves of this truth today does not—repeat not—mean that we intend to furl our flags, or to cease to march the streets, or to invade the taverns, cafés and public-houses with our literature, or to dispense with the Mercy Seat, or to silence all expressions of personal testimony or voluntary prayer in our public worship. These blessings are the outcome of God's gracious dealings with us, and are not to be wrapped up in a napkin and hidden in the ground.

We would share these insights into the proclamation of the gospel with the Church at large. This we can do in utter loyalty to our first Article of Faith which declares that "the Scriptures ... only constitute the divine rule of Christian faith and practice." There we find our essential guidelines. The content of the Christian gospel is there and the spirit of our Christian fellowship is there—either detailed in specific teaching or mirrored in Christian example. Any definition of the Church must, therefore, be a New Testament definition—where it is set out not in terms of ecclesiastical structure but of a spiritual relationship. Members of the Church are those who are "incorporate in Christ Jesus" (Ephesians 1:1, N.E.B.). This is the one thing needful. The Church is the whole of the worshipping, witnessing Christian community throughout the centuries into whatever groupings, large or small, accepted or persecuted, wealthy or poor, her mem-

[7] Frederick de L. Booth-Tucker, *The Life of Mrs. Booth* I, p. 428.

bers may have been structured in the past or are governed in the present.

What makes the people of God one people is not any form of organization, however venerable or however authoritative, but the grace of the one God and Father of all, the presence of the only Saviour, and the outworking of the one Spirit in the life of each believer. It is this gift of God, mediated directly to each faithful heart, which joins the disciple to his living Head and, at the same time, to his brother in the Lord. "We, who are many, are one body in Christ, and severally members one of another" (Romans 12:5 R.V.). No ecclesiastical formula will effectively unite the disciple to his Master unless there is first this inner and spiritual bond. Having confessed with the mouth the Lord Jesus Christ and believed with the heart that God has raised Him from the dead, believers are incorporate in Him. He whom Christ has accepted, man cannot disown. What is more, no churchly action can subsequently make that follower of Christ more totally and truly a member of His Body than he is already by repentance and faith alone.

This pattern was set at the first council of Jerusalem in A.D. 50. A section of the Early Church felt strongly that the terms of acceptance for Gentile entrants should be modelled upon the way of life practised by Jewish believers, even though that dated from their pre-Christian days. Both circumcision and the food taboos were held to have been prescribed by God for His chosen people in perpetuity. Were they now to tamper with the faith once delivered—even in the interest of their mission to the Gentile world? In any case, would any Gentile seeker sincerely desiring to know the truth have any objection to these requirements since Jesus, whom he was being urged to accept as Saviour and Lord, was Himself a circumcised Jew? But Paul—a Hebrew of the Hebrews if ever there was one—had seen for himself how the door of faith had been opened to circumcised and uncircumcised alike. Nor was Peter behind his brother apostle in declaring that "through the grace of the Lord Jesus Christ we shall be saved, even as they" (Acts 15:11).

Once again, only one thing was needful. With the Church defined in these New Testament terms, Augustine's saying that outside the Church there is no salvation becomes logical—and acceptable. For the Church is that happy company of men and women who have responded in faith to the call of the gospel. That, and that alone, is their passport to membership. They are born "not of blood, nor of the will of the flesh, nor of the will of man, but of God" (John 1:13). No more, but no less, is asked by The Salvation Army of those who would be enrolled in its ranks as soldiers. In this we are on firm New Testament ground.

7

ARE WE GREAT ENOUGH
to move toward one another
as Christ moved toward us?

by Frederick Coutts

Published in pamphlet form by The Salvation
Army, International Headquarters, London,
1967. (Originally appeared in *The Officer,* an
address given at a united church service during
the week of prayer for Christian unity.)

**Receive ye one another, as Christ also re-
ceived us to the glory of God. (Romans 15:7)**

WITH these words, the Apostle Paul comes to the personal appeal which concludes the main part of his
inspired survey of the unifying power of the gospel. This
survey is known to us as the Epistle to the Romans, which
gospel the Apostle declares to be the power of God unto
salvation.

First and foremost, the Apostle sees this gospel as
reconciling God and man. Man in his perversity had erected
a barrier between God and himself which, on his side, he
was powerless to remove. Yet where sin abounded, grace

had much more abounded. In the divine mercy a new and living way had been opened whereby man could come boldly to the Father's throne. The sons of ignorance and night could now cry: Abba. The long-lost filial relationship could be restored.

Again, the Apostle sees the gospel as uniting man with man—in the test case of the first century, Jew with Gentile. Between the two a great gulf had yawned. "I will buy with you, sell with you, talk with you, walk with you, and so following; but I will not eat with you, drink with you, nor pray with you." But the gospel had broken down this middle wall of partition. Paul's reasoning could be summarized: you were a Gentile; I was a Jew. God has made us both Christian.

A Common Fellowship

And again, the same gospel united in a common fellowship believers of varying degrees of spiritual perception and judgment. The strong in the faith could enjoy fellowship with the weak. No differences of opinion need mar their unity in the Lord. Instead, they were to share and to bear one another's burdens. That is to say: believers of every hue were to accept each other in the Lord as He had accepted them. This do, and they would glorify God.

And how had Christ received them? We can answer that from our own experience for we know how He received us. To adapt Charlotte Elliott slightly:

> *Just as I am, Thou* didst *receive,*
> Didst *welcome, pardon, cleanse, relieve.*

When we were no more worthy to be called His sons He ran to meet us with the kiss of forgiveness, transforming our woebegone appearance with robe and ring and shoes and, as a masterstroke, doing it all to music. Now, said the Apostle, as freely and as generously as God for Christ's sake accepted you when, by everything in the rule book, you were not worth accepting, so accept one another. Spelling this out, this means that each of us—Presbyterian, Congregationalist, Methodist, Anglican, Friend, Roman Catholic, Orthodox, Baptist, Salvationist—is to be welcomed as he is for what he is. He is a man in Christ. The Spirit bids us welcome him as a brother beloved.

I must add that no one should applaud this New Testament directive too quickly or too lightly. In reality this is a hard saying—especially when translating this principle into practice. For us to accept one another as we now are rules out the possibility of any hard ecclesiastical bargaining. That is to say, to work for the kind of compromise born of the negotiating table that if you will abandon your claim to "a," I will forgo my right to "b." For example, if all references to the Clarendon Code of 1661 are omitted from church histories published by the Saint Andrew Press, then the S.P.C.K. would return the delicate compliment by eliminating from their publications any derogatory references to the National Covenant of 1638. More bluntly: if you will waive the use of incense I will disavow the tambourine. Both, by the way, were features of Old Testament worship.

But in the shape of things to come we are not seeking a kind of lowest common denominator of Christian faith and practice. In the interests of unity no church should be called upon to deny that movement of the Spirit of God which brought her into being, nor to repudiate those insights to which she felt—and, if she be a living church—still feels herself called upon to witness. A church of the future in which the Methodist participants had forgotten the hymns of Charles Wesley, or the Presbyterians the time-honored supremacy of the word, or Salvationists their zeal for souls, would be a church from which the glory had departed. Our present divisions would be preferable—and, in my judgment, more serviceable—to God than such an emasculated body. The whole would be less than the sum of its parts—which would be intellectually absurd and spiritually calamitous.

Forget Superiorities

For if we are to receive one another as Christ received us, then we must forget our imagined superiorities—our historical superiorities, for example, which can be a besetting temptation for the older communions; our fancied spiritual superiorities, a besetting temptation of the younger bodies, including my own. I may not say to anyone who calls Jesus Lord—and none can do so save by the Spirit—your worship is defective. And, by the same token, nor may anyone say to me—because you have not taken part in this particular ceremony you are none of His.

Christ's Example

Unless it could be—and is this only a dream?—that in receiving one another we would remember not only how Christ received us, that is, as we were for what we were, but what He did in order so to receive us. For however we interpret those figures of speech by which we describe the relationship between the Father and the Son, it remains true that He who was rich for our sakes became poor. He who thought it not robbery to be equal with God made Himself of no reputation and took upon Himself the form of a servant and was made in the likeness of men. To repeat myself: He met us where we were as we were. He took on Him the seed of Abraham, being made in all things like unto His brethren. J. B. Phillips summed it up in the word that He stripped Himself of all privilege.

Does the hour find our churches great enough for that? To move toward one another as Christ moved toward us, as in divine generosity He accepted us as we were, sinful men whose only virtue was the grace of penitence? Penitence and acceptance; acceptance and penitence—are not these the root notes upon which any future harmonious relationships between Christian bodies alone can be based?

Already Begun

Before, like the rich young ruler, we turn away sorrrowful—for the churches have great possessions, of historical prestige, of ecclesiastical status—ought we not to remember that in a small way we have already begun to act like this?

We have begun to act like this with our praise. I do not suppose your hymn books differ radically from my song book, but when I open to the pages on the Atonement, I find Isaac Watts next to Frederick Faber, who is next to Paulus Gerhardt, who is next to George Bennard. And when I turn to the nature of the gracious God, there stands John Henry Newman next to Joachim Neander next to James Montgomery next to Charles Wesley.

We have begun to act like this in our thinking—for when we turn to our bookshelves in the hope that they may lighten our intellectual darkness, we do not first regard an author's churchmanship. Thielicke and Trueblood and Temple stand side by side. All highly irregular, without doubt. But it is acceptance—and every new act of acceptance of the unqualified universality of the gospel is accompanied by a deepening sense of penitence for past blindness whether intentional or unintentional.

We have begun to act like this with our witnessing. The many Christian fellowships in the city of London and elsewhere testify to a unity of spirit which transcends our ecclesiastical barriers. The same can be said of the Christian unions found in our comprehensive and grammar schools; and of the House of Commons Christian Fellowship; and of the unity of support—even though partial—given to the Billy Graham campaign at Earls Court.

Practicing Unity

In October 1965, I took part in an open-air gathering held on a Saturday at noon in Union Square, San Francisco. This is perhaps one of the busiest parts of the city and this certainly is one of the busiest hours. This religious meeting commenced with the local monsignor offering the invocation and concluded with the benediction pronounced by the President of the California State Baptist Association. I said my piece in the middle and was not conscious of bowing either to the right or to the left—though which was right and which left I leave you to say. But let there be no doubt—Jesus Christ was preached. And there were tambourines! And bands! And flags!

With much greater seriousness, when the call is to stand up and be counted in face of the foe, the thin red line may exhibit an untidy variety of uniforms but the spirit is one—as can be confirmed by reading either *Three Winters Cold, Captive in Korea* or *Valiant Dust.*

We have begun to act like this with our serving. Those who try to help the alcoholic (or the unwed mother, the social misfit) know that the first approach is not to ask his qualifications for being assisted—for he has none save his great need; but to accept him as he is, and this without a word of reproach or a trace of self-righteousness, and yet, so delicate is the balance, without in the least condoning his misconduct.

As by grace the saints so receive the sinner, may they not by virtue of the same all-sufficient grace receive one another in unconditional fellowship in the Lord?

To act like this would be—as the text suggests—to act to the glory of God.

8

The Founders and the Sacraments

by Harry Dean

From *Another Harvest of the Years.* Published by The Salvation Army, International Headquarters, London, 1975.

A PICTURE of William Booth in the popular mind is often of an eccentric, different from the rest of Christendom. This is entirely false; at heart he was conservative, yet driven by an urgent concern for the salvation of men untouched by ordinary religious effort.

Originally he had no desire or intention to found an organization. In early Christian Mission days he sent his converts to the churches, only to discover that those who went were not always welcome; others, feeling out of place in such a setting, had no desire to go at all, and in any case he soon needed all converts to evangelize their fellows. This situation necessitated the founding of a Movement.

Most innovations were forced upon William Booth by those near to him. Regarding the title "General" as pretentious, he insisted that on all official forms it should come after, not before, his name. He was also a reluctant convert to the wearing of uniform, particularly for himself. In spite of his later well-known question, "Why should the devil have all the best tunes?" he had to be won over to the use of secular airs for religious purposes.

William Booth was baptized into the Anglican communion; in the discharge of his duties as an ordained Methodist minister he administered the recognized Christian sacraments, and continued this in The Christian Mission and The Salvation Army. To quote from *The History of The Salvation Army,* volume II.

> Numerous instances of the administration of the sacrament by officers, men and women, are to be found in reports till well into 1881. A correspondent of the Nonconformist and Independent *(February 9, 1882)* called attention to the fact that in The Salvation Army the sacrament had for the first time in the history of the Church been administered *by* women.

In view of these facts the Army's attitude toward the sacraments becomes of considerable interest. It began in the mind of Catherine Booth, prompted by the General's secretary, George Scott Railton. Both of these strong personalities had a fear of formalism; then as now, much that passed for Christianity was primarily an observance of outward ritual. Catherine Booth and Railton wanted to put The Salvation Army on its guard against this ever-present danger.

Consistent with his general viewpoint on other matters, William Booth's attitude to the sacraments was that of a practical man. Constantly he asked: "Will the adoption of this idea, or the abandonment of that method, help or hinder the salvation war?" He had no desire to be out of step with other Christian denominations; his course was determined by desire to fulfil his God-given task.

When Catherine Booth and Railton brought pressure to bear upon the Founder regarding the sacraments, four facts were weighed:

(1) The vital Christian experience of the Society of Friends seemed an unanswerable argument that it was possible to live the Christian life without sacramental aids.

(2) Differing views and practices relating to the sacraments had always been a divisive influence among Christians.

(3) Administration created two problems:

    (a) The sacraments had been linked, in the main, with systems necessitating a separate priesthood for their administration; this suggested a double standard for Christians, and contradicted New Testament emphasis on the "priesthood of all believers."

    (b) There was the officiation by women. This had actually happened already, but had it become an established feature of Salvation Army practice it might prove a greater offence to many devout Christians than the Founder's decision to set aside sacraments altogether. Moreover, William Booth was not willing to surrender the principle of the perfect equality of men and women in every activity of the Kingdom of Christ.

(4) Many converts had been drunkards. What kind of wine would not revive the desire of former habits from which they had so recently been delivered? This matter proved persistently troublesome; unfermented wine was then unobtainable.

After much deliberation and consultation with his eldest son, Bramwell (the last offficer to administer the Lord's Supper within the Movement and who admitted to a great reluctance in accepting his father's final decision), the Founder ruled that, as the sacraments were symbols of spiritual truth and experience, Salvationists would henceforth seek only the substance and not rely upon the shadow.

Since the Army's earliest days the attitude has been positive rather than negative. In conversation with Henry S. Lunn, William booth said: "We never declaim against the sacraments. We are anxious not to destroy the confidence of Christian people in institutions which are helpful to them."

The stand he took was on the essentially spiritual nature of the Christian faith, but when asked if he would be willing to sanction his soldiers being baptized and partaking of the Lord's Supper if they so desired, his answer was an unqualified affirmative. An answer which years later was endorsed by his son Bramwell:

> Any soldier who declared a serious conviction in the matter and desired to participate—and this is still the law amongst us—could receive a recommendation to go to some other body for the purpose of partaking. (Echoes and Memories.)

What has troubled so many Christians in regard to the non-observance of the sacraments by the Society of Friends and The Salvation Army is the conviction that the sacraments were instituted by our Lord. They therefore feel it incumbent upon them to give due consideration to His commands. The evidence of the New Testament is not as conclusive as is commonly imagined. William Booth did not accept that Jesus had given any hard and fast instructions in regard to the Lord's Supper or baptism. He affirmed:

> If I believed that my Lord Jesus Christ required of me that I should take so many pieces of bread and so much wine every day of my life, I should unhesitatingly carry out His commands. There is nothing that I am conscious of that He requires me to do that I leave undone.

He went on to point out that there were many observances in the Early Church that Christendom later did not regard as binding, and he felt it legitimate to put the two generally recognized sacraments into the same category.

Centuries previously Erasmus had written:

> Read the New Testament as a whole; you will find no ceremonies. Ceremonies cause differences; charity fosters peace. Christ knows no commandment but charity.

And a Baptist scholar of more recent date, Dr. T. R. Glover: "There is a growing consensus of opinion among independent scholars that Jesus instituted no sacraments."

In the Acts of the Apostles there is early reference to "the breaking of bread," but no suggestion that this was a sacramental meal, and no reference to wine being associated with the bread.

> In the light of the evidence which scholarship affords (to quote Dr. Nathaniel Micklem), it seems probable that at the Last Supper Christ instituted no new rite. The normal type of the Eucharist, I take to be such gatherings as when, in the evening after the day's work was done, the disciples would gather round Him, and He, as master and head of the household, would ... offer thanks for the gifts of food ... and pass round the cup.

The *sacramental* Lord's Supper is a later development, and 1 Corinthians 11 shows this taking place in the Church at Corinth and reveals that in the Apostolic period developing ritual immediately becomes the occasion for division and strife.

It is generally recognized that the "mystery religions" of the first and second centuries had some influence upon the evolution of the primitive "love feast" to the highly developed rite of the Lord's Supper, and the pagan custom of administering oaths to soldiers was that which gave us the term "sacrament."

On these "mystery religions" the verdict has been passed that "they lent themselves too easily to externalism by an exaggerated importance of ritual ... they confused the physical symbol and the religious experience." There is a natural tendency in the human heart to place too great an importance upon ritual.

Further, the Founder's attitude to the sacraments was in keeping with Jesus' attitude to the Mosaic Law. Our Lord's emphasis was on the inwardness of religion. He declared that it is not what a man eats and drinks that defiles or sanctifies; the condition of the inner life is all-important and, in order to worship God, man needs nothing more than utter sincerity. When asked about the essence of the Jewish Law, He did not dwell upon its legal or ceremonial aspects. To His mind, whole-hearted love for God involving, as it must, the loving of one's fellows, was the crux; His commandment is that we love one another.

An experience of encounter and communion with God makes superfluous all ceremonial; Christ meets every spiritual need, with or without the use of external rites. His grace is not channelled in this way or that, but flows out to meet spiritual need wherever and whenever there is an awareness of that need.

Communion is of the spirit; therefore, as the sacramentalist would agree, to receive spiritual nourishment the soul must rise above the elements.

During the early days of the Army in India a reporter wrote:

> *The Salvationists never for a moment lay aside their consciousness that they are in the immediate presence of the Deity. They never quit it. They are as close to His feet while singing a song, beating a drum, or talking to the crowd, as when prostrate in prayer.*

The Salvationist accepts the message of the Lord to the Church in Laodicea: "Behold I stand at the door and knock; if any man hear My voice, and open the door, I will come in to him, and will sup with him, and he with Me."

9

The Sacraments of the Churches

by Frederick Coutts

From *The Salvation Army in Relation to the Church.* Published by The Salvation Army, International Headquarters, London, 1978.

THE meaning and observance of the sacraments have been for centuries matters of debate and difference between Christian believers. All who write or speak on the subject must therefore take the utmost care to avoid giving needless offence.

Though The Salvation Army does not observe the sacraments—of which there are traditionally seven, though two, baptism and the Lord's Supper, are most widely practiced in Protestant churches—we are not "against" them. Following our time-honored custom never to reflect on the practices of any other church, we never say—and have never said—anything hostile to their observance. There is nothing in our discipline which forbids either officer or soldier from sharing in the sacraments, though it is part of our teaching that the over-riding concern of Salvationists will be personally to experience that inward spiritual grace to which the sacraments testify. More than eighty years ago the Founder said: "We never declaim against them. ... We are anxious not to destroy the confidence of Christian people in any institutions which are helpful to them."[1]

General Bramwell Booth has recalled that when, as a lad, he began to take an active part in the work of The Christian Mission, "the Lord's Supper was administered monthly ... to all members of the Mission and to such other Christian friends known to be in good standing and who desired to join with us."[2] In March 1882, with the blessing of Archbishop Thomson, four hundred Salvationists in full uniform attended a celebration of Holy Communion at St. Peter's Holgate.[3] For at least four years, from 1880 onward, corps frequently marched to the local parish church, headed by members of the clergy and a surpliced choir.[4]

However, these gestures of goodwill provoked some unease on both sides. A number of the clergy in York protested that the St. Peter's service was a "defamation." Others were unwilling to offer the sacrament to those who had not been confirmed—and few Salvationists had been. Occasionally, a preacher sought to "improve" the occasion by urging the observances of the church upon the uniformed congregation. Thus there were some questionings in Army ranks as well. It was unthinkable that we should offer fermented wine to converts who had but recently been delivered from the curse of alcoholism. But what was to be offered instead? Water was preferable to any artificial concoction.

Further, who should offer the elements? Some of the members of the Christian Mission deliberately absented themselves unless the station evangelists—of whom a number were women—presided at the Lord's table. Even the

---

[1] William Booth to Sir Henry Lunn, *The Review of the Churches*, April 1895.

[2] Bramwell Booth, *Echoes and Memories* (Hodder & Stoughton, paperback), p. 201.

[3] Owen Chadwick, *The Victorian Church* (A. & C. Black), Pt. II, p. 295.

[4] Robert Sandall, *The History of The Salvation Army* (Nelson), II, p. 137ff.

suggestion that a woman might administer the sacraments was unwelcome—as it still is to some today. And even if all these difficulties had been overcome, would the Lord's Supper, as held in an unhallowed factory-building-turned-Salvation-Army-barracks by (in ecclesiastical eyes) an unordained layman, be recognized as valid by the historic churches?

The original evangelical impulse which had given birth to The Salvation Army brought its own solution. What was even more important than the observance of a ceremony, however ancient, was the inward possession of that spiritual grace of which the ceremony was an outward sign. The bread and the wine could be offered—and accepted—and yet the worshipper be unaware of the presence and power of the living Christ in his heart. Yet he who personally knows the divine presence has no need of the mediating elements. He possesses the substance of which they are the shadow.

It is to this inwardness of true religion that The Salvation Army has ever sought to testify. "No resolutions, religious ceremonies or pious feelings," said William Booth, "can make men good. ... There is no hope for permanent amendment without a change of heart. God is the Author of this change."

Subsequent scholarship has lent support to this emphasis. There is room for two major authorities to be quoted.

"We have seen," the Lady Margaret Professor of Divinity at the University of Oxford has written, "that there are some Christian groups that have discarded the commonly accepted sacraments. It is not to be denied that grace operates in them too, for the operation of the divine Spirit is not confined to the recognized sacraments. ... It may even be that these groups constitute a warning against the overprizing of sacramental forms."[5]

A similar note is sounded by Emil Brunner in *The Misunderstanding of the Church* (Lutterworth Press).

[5] *Principles of Christian Theology* (S.C.M.), p. 364.

> *Intimately as these two sacraments are associated with the saving events in Christ, yet ... they are not unconditionally necessary to salvation. In asserting their unconditional necessity to salvation, we should be contradicting the witness of the New Testament. One can speak of salvation in Christ apart from these two rites. One can believe in Christ and in salvation without sharing in these rites. The community of Jesus does not first become a reality through them; it already is a reality. ...*
>
> *The "where two or three are gathered together in My name, there am I" is still valid and real where there is no celebration of the Lord's Supper. ... The decisive test of one's belonging to Christ is not reception by baptism, nor partaking in the Lord's Supper, but solely and exclusively a union with Christ through faith which shows itself active in love.*

This is well said, for the Salvationist believes in the Real Presence as earnestly as any churchman. Indeed, it would be impossible to engage, for example, in a downtown open-air meeting, or hold a worship service in one of the hundreds of men's and women's shelters strategically placed across the globe, without the faith that the risen Lord is livingly present.

There are, of course, very earnest believers who reproach us for our non-observance of the sacraments. With the Quakers, we have been compared to a man who chooses to box with one hand tied behind his back.[6] The comparison is somewhat inept. The Salvationist does not fight as one who beats the air. Far from being limited to the periodic observance of a special rite in order to renew his spiritual strength, he knows that he can find grace to help in any setting at any time of need. To the heart of faith the Lord is ever at hand—as truly and powerfully present as when the Host is elevated or the elements distributed. To the praise of God, and that alone, we testify that this is as much a fact in our public assemblies as in our private devotions.

This may be agreed by some who nevertheless feel that no direct command of our Lord should be disobeyed. This is an understandable point of view which will never lose its

[6] J. R. Macphail, *The Way, the Truth and the Life*, p. 84.

validity. But since the days of Westcott and Hort it has been widely agreed that the words of institution in Luke 22:19*(b)* and 20 are an addition which may have been brought in from 1 Corinthians 11:24*(b)* and 27.[7] The New English Bible places these sentences in a footnote. They do not appear in Mark's account of the Last Supper, nor in Matthew's. As William Booth reminded Sir Henry Lunn in the conversation already mentioned, the Gospel of John says nothing at all about the bread and wine but quotes what Jesus said about the foot washing. If the Lord's Supper possessed so central and essential a place in the life of the Spirit, does it not provoke reflection that there is but one direct reference to the words of institution in the whole of the New Testament?[8]

We can speak with this freedom because we profoundly believe in, and are ever seeking to experience, the spiritual realities of which the sacraments are the sign. Nor is there any substance in the charge that for the historic sacraments we have substituted our own.

This is not true. We have a few simple forms of spiritual affirmation, but have never held the view that they are vehicles of a grace obtainable in no other way.

The Mercy Seat, or Penitent-form, holds a time-honored place in our evangelical work. But we have never taught that a penitent must kneel at the Mercy Seat in order to be converted. He can kneel anywhere—at his kitchen table, at his bedside, at the chair or bench on which he has been sitting in the Army hall. "I carry a Penitent-form around in my heart," was one of Brengle's greatest sayings, "and whenever I feel the need I kneel there." A Mercy Seat can be improvised. In a public hall a row of chairs can be turned around to face the congregation—and there is the Mercy Seat. In an open-air meeting the drum can be laid on its

[7] *The Staff Review,* April 1927, p. 191ff.
[8] Major Clifford Kew, "The Sacraments: Are They Essential?" *The Officer,* March-June 1978. These four studies deal illuminatingly with this very point.

side—and again there is the Mercy Seat. More than one Army officer has prayed for the salvation of a man's soul standing by the bar of a public house. Any situation is sacramental where a man is seeking God and where God is meeting the seeker.

Respectfully it may be said that the "sacraments" which a Salvationist celebrates far exceed the declared institutions of the churches. The biblical truth is that we can meet with God and receive His grace at every end and turn. We therefore propose, as God shall help us, to stand fast in the liberty wherewith Christ has set us free.

As William Cowper wrote:

> *Jesus, where'er Thy people meet,*
> *There they behold the Mercy Seat;*
> *Where'er they seek Thee Thou art found,*
> *And every place is hallowed ground.*

10

The Structure of the Church

by Frederick Coutts

From *The Salvation Army in Relation to the Church*. Published by The Salvation Army, International Headquarters, London, 1978.

IF it is agreed that the Church consists of those who are "claimed by God for his own" (I Peter 2:9 N.E.B.), the next question has to do with the development and ordering of the corporate life of the people of God.

To confess that "Jesus Christ is Lord, to the glory of God the Father" (Philippians 2: 11) was the essential affirmation asked of those who desired to belong to the household of faith. But no such firm pattern was laid down for the increase of that household. The witness of the first believers was clear and plain. It was to the power of the Resurrection and the Lordship of Christ. But the proclamation of that message followed no fixed design, neither was there any single set procedure laid down for the appointment of the Church's leaders. At the beginning the apostles carried the burdens of that leadership—with Peter outstanding. But it was not long before other men and women assumed various responsibilities, both large and small, in almost an *ad hoc* fashion.

Doubtless the Acts of the Apostles gives but a selective account of the activities of the Early Church. But, with the addition of such incidental references as occur in the New Testament epistles, it is the only record we have—and must therefore take pride of place.

It could also rightly be argued that the churches of the Mediterranean world developed in various areas and at varying speeds what is held by the episcopal churches to be the appointed order of bishop, priest and deacon. But nowhere in the Acts of the Apostles do the Twelve ordain their successors. Indeed when James, son of Zebedee, was martyred (Acts 12:2), no successor was named. The New Testament provides no one pattern to be followed universally and in perpetuity. The picture given in Scripture is one of freedom in the Spirit. That is to say, the unity of the body, of which Christ is the Head, was preserved, but the members, being many, each fulfilled his own office as the Spirit led. There was unity in diversity and diversity in unity—and illustrations of both kinds can be noted.

For example, there was at times the laying on of hands. The apostles so confirmed the popular choice of seven men of honest report to supervise the distribution of church relief in Jerusalem. But these were not their successors, nor is there any record of the Seven naming their successors. Nor were there any further ordinations to any office by the Twelve.

Again, "prophets and teachers" from the Christian community in Antioch—not any member of the Twelve—laid hands on Barnabas and Saul and bade them Godspeed on their mission which led to the establishment of a number of churches in the Roman province of Galatia. By contrast, who founded the church in Rome, or when, is a matter of tradition. Peter's destination is not even hinted when he left Jerusalem (Acts 12:17). All we know from Scripture is that, when Paul reached the imperial capital, believers were waiting to greet him.

Yet again, does not the life and work of Paul himself set a

question mark against any rigid theory of apostolic succession? He was not ordained by any of the Twelve, though in due season he was given the right hand of fellowship by Peter, James and John on the understanding that he would pursue his mission to the Gentiles while they would do the same among the Jews. But Paul owed his welcome in the first place to the generous heart and mind of Barnabas—a Cypriot Jew, who vouched for him in Damascus and then rescued him from obscurity in Tarsus.

So in the field of evangelism, Philip—deacon not apostle—told the Ethiopian court official the good news about Jesus and then baptized him in a desert stream. But the Holy Spirit came upon Cornelius and his friends before Peter had finished speaking, and certainly without waiting for baptism at his hands.

It may be argued—and rightly—that no general rule can be established on the basis of isolated incidents. That is just the point. In the churches of the New Testament there was no universal obligation—save (as already noted) that of a confession of faith in Jesus as Saviour and Lord. Yet men whose ministry was—in the light of later dogma—highly irregular, were used of God to communicate the apostolic message because they possessed the apostolic spirit. Just as the link which bound the convert to the Church was spiritual in nature—that is, the testimony of the inward assurance, so was the qualification needed for the proclamation of the apostolic message.

This was the line taken by F. J. Hort, close Cambridge neighbor of Bishop Westcott who shared in the conversations with William Booth: "The true succession [he wrote] is through the Spirit. The apostolic succession means nothing more or less than the continual call of men to service by Christ Himself. No ceremony avails to effect it. The ministry of the New Testament is one of mission."

This is the considered judgment of John Macquarrie, Lady

Margaret Professor of Divinity at the University of Oxford.

There is no single criterion for the apostolic ministry. In the past, great stress has been laid ... on one particular constitutive element in this ministry, namely, its transmission through the succession of bishops, a transmission symbolized by the laying on of hands. This is undoubtedly a part in the fullness of the ministry, and an important part. But it is not the whole, or the only element in apostolic succession. Equally important is the transmission of apostolic truth. In some cases, this apostolic teaching in its essentials continues ... and, in such cases, one cannot deny any important continuity with the apostles.[1]

One further quotation is to the point.

The historic episcopate, however venerable and valuable, is strictly a post-New Testament development, both as an institution and as a subject for theological reflection; and all views which posit as an historical fact the transmission through it of the apostolic ministerial commission, or which regards this succession as part of the given structural essence of Christ's Church, and so of the apostolic faith concerning that Church, remain unverifiable hypotheses.[2]

As Frederic Myers wrote:

... He takes and He refuses
Finds Him ambassadors whom men deny,
Wise one nor mighty for His saints He chooses ...

This is clear from the divine choice and from the divine use in practice as well. Not all whom our Lord commissioned before His return to the Father seem to have been of equal capacity or were used in equal measure. Some disappear from the scriptural scene. Others are never mentioned at all. And of those to whom reference is made, some play a minor part. For example, at the opening of the Acts of the Apostles, John seems to have played a subordinate role to Peter. At any rate, it was the big fisherman who did the talking (Acts 3:

[1] *Christian Unity and Christian Diversity* (S.C.M.), p. 62.
[2] Church Information Service, *Intercommunion Today*, p. 57.

4; 3: 6; 4: 8; 8: 20), though John doubtless came into his own later on in life.

But even Peter vanished from view after his narrow escape from martyrdom. "Report this to James," was his instruction. "Then he left the house and went off elsewhere" (Acts 12: 17, N.E.B.). We can piece together his later movements from isolated references—such as his visit to Antioch (Galatians 2: 11), a possible presence at Corinth (1 Corinthians 1: 12), his missionary work in the provinces of Asia Minor (1 Peter 1: 1). He shared in the Jerusalem Council (Acts 15: 7), but it was left to James, the Lord's brother, to summarize the Council's discussion and to say how their decisions were to be conveyed to the churches (Acts 15: 13). We do not know who appointed James to this headship, but he was still in charge when Paul visited Jerusalem for the last time (Acts 21: 18).

In all this there was a wide variety of activity and of leadership, which is best described as the response of the Church, as guided by the Spirit, to the needs of the hour—to the immense gain of the work of God. Order and structure were fluid. "It seemed good to the Holy Ghost and to us ..." was the manner of decision taking. God has ever fulfilled Himself in many ways.

Nor does this contradict our Lord's prayer for His disciples—"that they all may be one" (John 17: 21). The phrase is often sincerely uttered by those to whom the unity of the Church is particularly dear. With every respect, however, it may be said that these words have nothing to do with what are called schemes for organic union. This is not a prayer for unity of organization, nor can the "oneness" to which the phrase refers be brought about by administrative changes. The words refer to a spiritual unity as is manifest in the "oneness" of the Father, Son and Holy Spirit. There is no richer diversity than is manifest by the Trinity, yet no diversity is more completely a unity, with Father, Son and Holy Spirit sharing every act of thought, will and feeling.

To sum up: with F. J. Hort (and others)—we believe that "the true succession is through the Spirit." There is no biblical or theological reason why The Salvation Army, moved by the Spirit, should not accept, train and use in the service of God those who profess themselves called to serve as officers of The Salvation Army. Such must give proof of their calling but, where a sense of vocation, personal godliness and intellectual capacity are manifest, none—neither man nor woman—needs be debarred from fulfilling their divine calling.

As General Bramwell Booth wrote: "We believe that our Lord Jesus Christ has called us into His Church of the redeemed, that our call has not been by man or the will of man, but by the Holy Spirit of God ... and that our officers are ... endowed by His grace, assured of His guidance, confirmed by His word and commissioned by His Spirit to represent Him to the whole world."

11

Churches Adopting Army's Methods

(An Editorial)

From *The Staff Review,* November 1929. Published by The Salvation Army, International Headquarters, London.

HOW wistfully many earnest spirits in the churches are turning towards the Army and asking the secret of its progress amidst the almost universal signs of decline experienced by other religious denominations! Not long since we published in these pages an article reviewing several books, written by eminent Roman Catholic leaders during the last few years, which drew attention to the Army's wise marshalling of its lay forces, and advocated certain measures for organizing the rank and file of Catholicism in frank imitation of the Army. Now we have a Primitive Methodist minister writing two articles in the official organ of the denomination, under the caption: "The Salvation Army and the churches." In these we have again an endorsement of the practical value of the Army's methods of work, and a plea for their adoption by the churches! Yet how often it is necessary to urge officers to *"Do The Salvation Army and do it in The Salvation Army way!"*

The writer remarks with wondering admiration that "After fifty years of marvellous growth and achievement, after attaining world-wide popularity and after receiving the patronage of kings, emperors and presidents, it still throbs with a passion for souls and is still concerned with 'publicans and sinners.' It has not yet become too respectable to wage war in the open air, to carry its flag into foul slum and dark alley. Best of all it has not lost its power to reach and save the very worst of men....

"But the Army is confronted with a new situation. It has now to cater for a vast host of Christian people of the second and third generations whose needs are not the same as those of the unredeemed masses outside. The Army has now not only to seek lost 'publicans and sinners' but to feed the lambs and sheep inside the fold.

"We do not wish to exalt the Army as the ideal Christian Society," the writer continues, "but we ask whether something of that which is best in the methods and spirit of that great organization could not be made vital and integral parts of the life and witness of the churches?"

The writer in his second article tells how he organized "a number of keen, spiritually-minded young men and women with fine potentialities for Christian service," into what he terms "something like a Salvation Army Company" to assist him in a week's Spiritual Advance Campaign at each of the four churches in his circuit.

"These campaigns were very successful. Many conversions were witnessed. The young campaigners would speak, testify, plead, pray, or sing at my request. I often took no part in the services until after the sermon, when I would take charge of the delicate operation known as 'drawing in the nets.' On their own initiative, too, these young people held improvised prayer meetings in the homes of the sick and conducted open-air meetings at street corners or by lamp-posts. They visited from house to house, inviting people to the services, and spared no efforts to persuade some to attend. It was marvellous to see how God used them. As we fought together I saw visions of infinite possibilities in wider fields.

"I had long been impressed with the immense advantages The Salvation Army possesses for aggressive evangelistic work amongst the masses—especially in the open air. The band, the flag, the uniforms, the orderly marching, the sublimated militarism of a Salvation Army company at its best, are of tremendous help in the work.

"Not only do these things help in attracting, holding, and moving a crowd, they are also a great inspiration to those engaged in the work. It is work which calls for courage, endurance and the glowing heart. What could be more inspiriting than to find oneself marching to the conflict in a company of uniformed Soldiers of the Cross, with a band playing stirring music and a banner floating aloft?

"Why should these undoubted advantages be confined to The Salvation Army? Why should there not be something like a Salvation Army company in all our larger churches?"

My purpose in quoting at length from these two articles is the hope that the lesson of them may not be lost upon some officers who seem bent upon approaching as near as may be in their meetings to the manner and methods of the parson, what time many sensible parsons are envying us our happy freedom from the restraints of religious convention and trying, as the writer I have quoted is doing, to shake themselves free. These comrades of ours speak of their addresses as "sermons," of their meetings as "services"; they are keen on being invited to become members of the "Ministers' Fraternals" in the town or city in which their headquarters is located. They tend to become more and more sedately parsonic, and less and less Salvation Army. They insist much on "the need of reverence in public worship" as if the freedom and abandon of the Spirit-filled children of God were incompatible with true reverence in the presence of their Heavenly Father.

12

The World Council of Churches

by Albert Orsborn

From *The Officer*, March/April 1954. Published by The Salvation Army, International Headquarters, London.

YOU will have noticed that the Assembly of the World Council of Churches is to meet at Evanston, Illinois, U.S.A., in August next. The Salvation Army will be represented by a delegation of six officers who will be fully briefed concerning Army policy on the main issues to be raised and discussed. Their instructions will be prepared in consultation with myself, and in full session of the forthcoming Commissioners' Conference, which will follow the High Council and the election of my successor. Our delegates will not participate in all the group discussions in the assembly. These precede and report back to the plenary sessions, which our delegation will attend in full strength. We anticipate being asked to participate in the group discussions for which we have opted: i.e. evangelism, social questions, international affairs, and the laity. Faith and order (belief and church organization), and inter-group relations, including racial and ethnic tensions, are other subjects which will arise in the plenary sessions.

You may ask, "Why are we there?" And, "What are we going to do or say?" These are proper questions. I should expect our officers to ask them, for the matter of Army relationships with the churches is, and always has been, of great importance, both to them and to us. It is known that in Britain, and in other lands, there were early-day attempts to persuade the Founder to consent to our Movement being organically joined with the Established Church. William Booth did not dismiss these suggestions without considering them. On the contrary, our history shows that he treated such proposals with great respect not failing to recognize the compliment they implied. Nevertheless he rejected them, and was led to maintain our separateness in our constitution, our government, and our activities. How wise he was! Nothing has occurred which would justify us in revising the Founder's decision. Then, why are we in the World Council of Churches?

We have been associated with the World Council of Churches from its very beginning. The late Commissioner A.G. Cunningham was our permanent representative, and ultimately became a valued member of the main Executive Committee. When he withdrew, I thought fit not to nominate anyone to take his place on the Executive Committee, but for the Army to remain in general membership.

There can be no question about our duty to maintain and cultivate friendship toward all Christians. That has always been our attitude toward the churches, even in the days when some of our fiercest and most bitter opposition came from them. To this day, we are still accepted by some churches only as social welfare workers; they do not admit our claim that we have within ourselves a corporate spiritual life, with its own authority, able to provide for our people all the services and rights exercised by a Church toward its members. But we are almost universally recognized as a religious denomination by governments, and for purposes of a national emergency—such as war services—or for convenience in designating our officers, they group us with the churches. That is as far as we wish to go in being known as a church. We are, and wish to remain, a Movement for the revival of religion, a permanent mission to the unconverted, one of the world's greatest missionary societies; but not an establishment, not a sect, not a church, except that we are a part of that body of Christ called "The Church Militant" and we shall be there, by His grace, with "The Church Triumphant." It therefore follows that we are friendly with all whom Christ has named His own, and for that primary reason we do not refuse fellowship with the World Council.

We are also in the Council that we may lend the experience and the testimony of the Army to those aims and purposes which are especially dear to the Salvationist. We find that members of the Council are pleased to have our contribution, because we are in touch with the people in so many different lands.

We are there to listen, and perhaps to learn. But we are not prepared to change or to modify our own particular and characteristic principles and methods. Not that we have been asked to do so. Not at all! But we may at some time come up to a definite issue on one or more of the matters I will mention. Should that situation arise, we will meet it. Meanwhile, there are many good things we can do. We can exchange visits with churches, for spiritual purposes. This is often done. We can make common cause with the churches on big social issues, where our principles and purposes are clearly harmonious with them, and where our headquarters so decides. We can join the group on big emergency questions, such as arise in war-time or in moments of national disaster. In some instances we can advantageously join with national or local church councils, with missionary councils in non-Christian lands and, of course, with the World Council. Each of these cases must be considered and decided by Territorial Headquarters or by International Headquarters, according to local conditions, for these vary a great deal in different lands, and it does not follow that we do the same thing everywhere.

But where do we stop? That is a great and most important question. Are you willing to follow me while I try briefly to answer it? I wish you would, for it is so important that our officers everywhere understand our freedoms and our distinctions, as well as our identity with others.

The Founder gave us a great freedom. Remember that! Let us not get into a state of mind that is disconnected from our own vital history. He came out from the churches, and stayed out, not because he was awkward and independent, not because he wanted to "boss his own show," but for deep and strong reasons of a spiritual nature. Let's pose one or two almost self-answering questions. We will not thrash them out, but just throw them on the screen and look at them.

Would we do better soul-winning, real Army work and Army building, by closer identification with the churches? Would this help us to get nearer the man in the street, or in the pubs or, as some say, the saloons? Has not our strength lain in our separateness? We are not large as compared with the statistical strength of some of the churches. This applies in all countries. But we are distinctive and specific. Are not the distinctions of The Salvation Army recognized and admitted by "John Citizen," who may be called "our man," indispensable to our survival? Would we not weaken ourselves by agreeing to any form of organic unity with other bodies? Certainly proportionate representation, which we have had to fight in so many countries, on so many issues— such as teaching in schools and the use of the radio—would leave us badly in the rear. God has given us a position and an influence in the world by far greater than our numbers: I have been jealous of this, and determined not to give it away.

The divisions among the churches are deep, and so far the noble experiment of the World Council has not changed them. It is not with any bitterness, and certainly not with the least despair, that one remarks that the United Nations and the United Churches are alike in that their coming together

90

reveals how far apart they are. What do I mean by this? And how does it affect us? I will tell you how I see these things, and I must confess I do not see how the Army can help in these particular matters, though I do most certainly see a danger of our being drawn into them to our own weakening and loss of time and effort.

For example, there is disagreement on the question of Authority—spelled with a capital 'A'. I refer, of course, to that spiritual authority which is partly moral and partly ecclesiastical. To which church does it belong, or does it belong to all equally? When the churches combine, by whose authority do they speak to their own members or to the outside world?

The Church of Rome makes no concessions to anyone on this question, and that is perhaps the main reason for her absence from this World Council. Within the Council there are many who would like to see Rome come in; but if she came in, many others would go out. So there is a division on this question of Authority, or Church discipline and order. We Salvationists believe that Jesus Christ confers His authority, His power, upon all those men and women whom He calls and commissions to His service. By that authority we have lived and worked; without it we would be lost.

Then there is the difference that exists within the Council on the meaning of "the churches" and "the Church." There are deep disagreements among the constituent churches on this very point. These disagreements are based on convictions held by good people, yet they make it hard for the various churches to create a "self" made up of those different bodies into one Church. The Council is not committed beforehand to any one of these many views; it is merely the place where they are discussed. It is certainly not of itself the re-united Church. It does not explicitly confess that it aims at organic unity, but it continually asserts that some day this issue must be faced, and it lays the obligation to do this on all who are members.

Another point is the difficulty of finding agreeable formulae by which the Council can make pronouncements to the world. Some months ago the Provisional Committee issued this statement:

> The Council considers itself responsible to Jesus Christ, the Head of the Church, to seek to know the will of God upon important issues which radically affect the Church and society, and thereafter in the Name of Christ, in dependence upon the Holy Spirit, and in penitence and faith, to call upon churches, governments or men in general, as the situation may require, to deal with a given historical issue, in the name of Christ and in the light of God's revelation in Jesus Christ the Lord.

But there are many who question either the wisdom of accepting such a responsibility, or even of recognizing it. The dangers and snares awaiting the churches attempting to deal with these complicated issues, which so often impinge upon politics and upon secular interests, are too evident to need stressing. Attempts, so far, to make pronouncements on such issues have ended in formulae which meant very little, and aroused neither comment nor controversy.

There are other divisive questions, such as that of comprehensiveness, i.e. the basis, the scope of the World Council of Churches. There are some who now stay outside who might be prepared to join if all doctrinal discussion and all corporate worship were dropped, and the Council became an organization for co-ordinating relief and "practical cooperation on the basis of natural law." If the Council were to move thus, it would lose many of the present members. And so on; there are other such issues. I will not belabor them. Thank you for reading thus far.

Now I will tell you what we do not want for the Army, and what we will not have:

> We do not favor organic unity with the churches. We feel we are able to do better work for God and man by remaining what we are, a simple, untrammelled Army of salvation.

> We can accept no discussion and no challenge to

our position on the sacraments. The Army's teaching on this matter is too well known to need repetition.

We cannot allow the effective ordination (commission) of our officers, including the women, to be challenged. We should never agree to their re-ordination at the hands of anyone.

We are not prepared to change our doctrine. True, it is not under challenge; but it might well be so at some future stage. We do not even feel under any obligation to defend or explain our doctrine to any who differ from it. Our eleven articles are fundamental to Salvationism, and cannot be changed.

We must preserve absolutely our world-wide missionary freedom; we could not accept "zoning." Our one International Army must be kept intact, always remembering that "churches" are not all alike, and have differing status in various countries.

We cannot allow ourselves to become involved in those so called "social" questions which in reality are political, and tend to bring religion into conflict with governments and parties, who are always only too willing to blame the Church for failures of secular schemes in which religion permits itself to become involved.

We cannot join anything which may tend to curb our spirit of aggression. We are already in danger of becoming too "set," a deadly danger which every officer must watch and guard against. Nothing, no union of any kind which increases our ecclesiasticism and reduces our enthusiasm must be allowed.

We must agree to nothing which might give our people the idea that it is all the same with us whether they are loyal to the Army or not, or which might suggest that we are not particular about building a stronger and a better Army from our converts.

We must not join any aims and purposes which

> *might have the effect of gradually changing the nature and aims of our training colleges. These are not merely educational or academic institutions. They are designed to be training schools where our first emphases are on religion, revivalism, soul-saving, with our own special hallmark on all who go through.*

Well, dear officer-reader, I beg your pardon for this rather lengthy and prosy article. I do assure you I write with conviction, after much thought, research, and prayer. I write because I wish you to know where we stand, where we will or will not move within the World Council. I regard this as one of the most important issues before us in this present day. I claim to know where I stand, in the light of our traditions, and our history. I hope you know also, and that you will pray for those who go to Evanston, that they be imbued with the spirit of good fellowship, and while not committing the Army to any change of policy, may make clear in what matters we will co-operate, and may learn the views of others. That is our purpose. May God bless all the members of His true Church upon earth, no matter what their communion, and give grace and strength to them to work for His kingdom.

13

The Army
and the
World Council of Churches

by Wilfred Kitching

From *The Officer*, September/October and November/December, 1961. Published by The Salvation Army, International Headquarters, London.

MY appointment of nine officers from the five continents to represent the Army at the Third Assembly of the World Council of Churches follows the tradition of fellowship and cooperation with other Christian bodies we have enjoyed from the Founder's days onward. We have ever been ready to support those who are sincerely striving to bring the Kingdom of Christ on earth and we have ever been grateful for the understanding our friends of the churches and their leaders have shown the Army's aims and methods.

The First Assembly of the World Council of Churches held at Amsterdam in 1948 initiated a new phase in ecumenical activities by bringing together bodies with which the Army had previously been associated— "faith and order," and "life and work" and many sectionalized inter-church activities. At Amsterdam we were represented by a delegation of five officers from different lands and at Evanston by six. The

Third Assembly taking place in New Delhi this year is expected to see a further formal union of two world-embracing bodies, the International Missionary Council and the World Council of Churches, with both of which again the Army has had long and close association, and on whose closer cooperation Salvationists will continue to pray God's blessing.

Our association with the International Missionary Council has been through our membership of Christian Councils associated with it in many lands. Of the World Council we have been a full member from its inception, provisionally planned in pre-war days but confirmed only in 1948 through the interruption of war. Our delegates to the assembly and our regular representatives on the Central Committee of the World Council of Churches have found much inspiration and goodwill accruing to the Army through this fellowship and the World Council of Churches on its part has always understood and valued the special contribution the Army has to make to the advance of the Kingdom. Our bond of fellowship is our common acceptance of Jesus Christ as God and Saviour and our determination to proclaim His Kingship to all the world.

Our delegates at the First Assembly of the World Council of Churches (at Amsterdam, 1948) were: Commissioner Marcel Allemand (Switzerland), Lieut.-Commissioner A. Beekhuis (Holland), Commissioner Geo. Bowyer (Great Britain), Commissioner A. G. Cunningham (I.H.Q.), and Commissioner Ernest Pugmire (U.S.A.).

To the Second Assembly (Evanston, U.S.A., 1954) we sent: Commissioner Claude Bates (U.S.A. Cent.), Colonel Joseph Dahya (India), Mrs. Commissioner Donald McMillan (U.S.A. East), Mrs. General Orsborn (Great Britain), Colonel Yasowo Segawa (Japan), and Commissioner Gordon Simpson (I.H.Q., London).

Our delegation at the Third Asembly (New Delhi, India, 1961) will be: Brigadier B. L. Benjamin (Pakistan), Colonel

Bramwell Cook (New Zealand), Senior-Major Jacobus A. Corputty (Indonesia), Lieut.-Commissioner Joseph Dahya (N.E. India), Commissioner Norman Marshall (National Commander, U.S.A.), Brigadier Jonah Munyi (East Africa), Colonel Donald Sanjivi (South India), Commissioner Reginald Woods (I.H.Q., London), and Colonel Tamiko Yamamuro (Japan). The Salvationist member of the Youth Delegation: Sister Prema Sanjivi (Madras).

Although the Army's position has been clear from the start, events like the New Delhi Assembly always bring to light those who have never been clear about what is the nature of our association with the ecumenical movement, and for this reason I have had a statement on the matter prepared for the guidance and use of Salvationists everywhere.

I pray that the act of reading this reminder in question and answer form of the simple facts will stimulate increased prayer for the onward march of the Church of Christ across a world under such heavy attack from the forces of darkness. Light is stronger than darkness and Jesus Christ is the Light of the World.

> *Jesus shall conquer,*
> *Lift up the strain!*
> *Evil shall perish*
> *And righteousness shall reign.*

Some Questions Answered

The appointment by the General of a strongly international group to represent the Army at the forthcoming Third Assembly of the World Council of Churches at New Delhi raises afresh a number of questions sometimes put to Salvationists.

1. What is The Salvation Army? William and Catherine

Booth and their helpers did not set out to create another church but to prosecute a vigorous mission to the churchless. In a course of lectures given nearly eighty years ago to a distinguished audience at a London Hotel, Catherine Booth mentioned that ninety per cent of the masses were said never to enter church, chapel or mission hall, and she claimed that anybody who believed in any kind of religion must see the awful necessity for some extraneous and irregular agency, adapted to reach this continent of dark, indifferent, infidel souls!

> *My dear husband was led especially to contemplate these masses. ... God showed him that between the churches and working classes, as a rule, there was a great gap; he saw that there was needed some instrumentality that would come between the two and take hold of the lower stratum, which, in the great majority of cases was uncared for and unthought of; and he set himself to do it in the East of London. God so wonderfully blessed him that the work soon began to grow of its own aggressive and expansive force. ... Some of the greatest reprobates in London ... came from seven, ten, and fifteen miles to those services, to look at ... some fighting, dog-fancying or pigeon-flying companion, who was reported to have been saved on the previous Sunday, and some of these got caught also. They...immediately became anxious for the salvation of their fellows. ... My husband would say: "If you can get anybody's kitchen or an old dancing saloon or penny gaff, I will get some of my working men to come and help you on Sundays, and you must do the rest yourselves." Thus little missions at Poplar, Canning Town, and other places were opened; and in this way the Christian Mission has grown into The Salvation Army!*

And in this way The Salvation Army swept around the world. "We had no more idea than anybody in this audience of what God was going to do with us," she said, "but we both had the conviction that He wanted to use us to help the masses in a way in which we could not be used in our denomination."

Years later, Catherine's son, the Army's second General, wrote: "There is one Church ... Of this, the Great Church of the Living God, we claim, and have ever claimed, that we of

The Salvation Army are an integral part and element—a living, fruit-bearing branch of the True Vine." This declaration finds an echo in an expression American Salvationists are particularly fond of when they say that our soldiers belong to "that part of the Church of Christ on earth known as The Salvation Army!"

To return to General Bramwell Booth: "We are in no way inferior, either to the saints who have gone before, or—though remaining separate from them even as one branch of the vine is separate from another—to the saints of the present," he wrote. "And our officers are equally with them, ministers in the Church of God, having received diversities of gifts but the one Spirit—endowed by His grace, assured of His guidance, confirmed by His word, and commissioned by the Holy Ghost to represent Him to the whole world."

"As the greater includes the less," wrote Commissioner F. L. Coutts in a recent issue of *Victory* (Australia), "it follows that Sydney Congress Hall is as much a 'church' as St. Stephen's. ... In each place, though in admittedly different ways, praise and prayer are offered, the word of God is proclaimed and there stands in the midst the One who has promised to be present where two or three are gathered in His name." Though we do not have some things many churches use, we do, as the Commissioner points out, "have certain God-blessed features which many churches lack, such as public testimony, free prayer, open-air activity ... and a vocabulary that speaks of the reality of the conflict between light and darkness." Our place as an Army is its drive for the churchless.

2. What has been the attitude of the Army to the churches and of the churches to the Army? There were many in the first days of the Army's battles who misunderstood its methods and misrepresented its motives; in fact it sometimes seemed that the secular press was more understanding of the Movement than the religious press. At the same time many famous leaders of many branches of religious thought showed great charity and generosity in acknowledging the sincerity and success of the Founders, and their view soon became general. From the start the Army made a point of not criticising other Christians even in refutation of slanders which might have been made against it. As the Founder told the Archbishop of Canterbury of that day: "We think we have a claim on your sympathy, because we do not seek to justify our existence by finding fault with you!" And his officers were told: "Rejoice in all the good done, by whomsoever it is done. Be glad whenever you find a good man or woman at work for God, and for the salvation of the people. Never try to find a hole in their coat, or pull them to pieces."

No Rivalry

The Army did not give up any of the great fundamental doctrines in order to attract the people but preached the biblical doctrines of the Fall, God's universal call to repentance, the need for justification by faith through our Lord Jesus Christ, the duty of a life of obedience, and the existence of Heaven and Hell, its chief mark of distinction being the sense of urgency with which it used every means to press the claims of the gospel upon the attention of men.

> We are one in our aim with the churches (the Army Mother declared). Our object is the enlightenment and salvation and exaltation of the people. ... We do not say, "Do it in our own way," only do it. Face the evil and do something. ... God only knows how deeply I desire that all godly men could present one common front to the foe, that we might be one in united effort. If this cannot be, let us all do our best. ... We do not hinder but help the churches ... We have the testimony of many of the bishops and clergy and ministers of all denominations to the stirring up of zeal and effort in the churches attributable to the wide-spread influence of our Movement. ...

At about the time the Army Mother was talking like this the then Archbishop of York (Dr. Thomson) was writing to the

Founder: "Some of us ... believe that you are moved by zeal for God, and not by a spirit of rivalry with the church, or any other agency for good, and they wish not to find themselves in needless antagonism with any in whom such principles and purposes prevail." Shortly afterwards the Church of England appointed a commission which opened negotiations with the Founder with a view to finding out if the Army could be linked up in union with that Church. If the Founder could have been convinced that this would not have slowed down the rate at which Salvationists were winning men for God in their chosen field this might have become one of the earliest acts of reunion in the country.

Goodwill From Church Leaders

From our earliest days we have had many evidences of the goodwill and understanding of church leaders. Bishop Lightfoot, a member of the commission referred to, wrote:

> *Shall we be satisfied with going on as hitherto, picking up one here and one there?...The Salvation Army, whatever may be its faults, has at least recalled to us the lost ideal of the work of the church, the universal compulsion of the souls of men.*

Dr. Benson, another member and afterward Archbishop of Canterbury, had a vision of the future in which he "saw the Army as a force—a force which would go far and carry much;" and subsequent events have abundantly proved that he was right. He once attended an officers' meeting at Clapton which developed into a prayer meeting of great power and liberty, and after watching for nearly an hour on his knees, he said to Bramwell Booth: "O, my dear brother, the Holy Spirit is with you!"

Dr. Davidson, who negotiated with the Founder on behalf of the Archbishop of Canterbury and afterward himself became Archbishop, wrote:

> *... after attending a large number of meetings of different kinds in various parts of London I thank God from my heart that He has*

raised up to proclaim His message of salvation the men and women who are now guiding the Army's work, and whose power of appealing to the hearts of their hearers is a gift from the Lord Himself. ...

Earlier, Archbishop Tait had sent a donation toward the purchase of the notorious Eagle Tavern which the Army converted into a center of salvation, and his successor "thanked God for every hand held out to help the sad and suffering and to rescue the fallen...." Dr. Liddon, a great pulpit figure of St. Paul's Cathedral, used to attend Bramwell Booth's holiness meetings in Whitechapel and take a hearty share in the singing, and enjoy the testimonies. Archdeacon Wilberforce entertained the Army Mother in his home, and Dr. Temple, another Archbishop, joined W. T. Stead's committee of investigation as chairman when the charge was made that the Army's "Maiden Tribute" purity campaign facts had been overstated. The Roman Catholic Cardinal Manning said that the spiritual desolation of London alone, let alone of England, would make The Salvation Army possible, and to the Founder he wrote, "You have gone down into the depths. Every living soul cost the most Precious Blood, and we ought to save it, even the worthless and the worst." From the earliest times and in every land the Army's patience in the face of misunderstanding or even persecution has been rewarded by a growth of friendship and co-operation with the churches.

3. What is the World Council of Churches? It is not a super-church. Nor is it a "World-Church." It does not exist to negotiate union between the churches. It is in fact a fellowship in which member organizations can discuss and pray together, seek to understand one another *and bear their own specific witness,* take counsel and common action where called for, and co-ordinate much of their thinking and effort.

From 1910 there was considerable development toward consultation and co-operation between the churches, and especially the movements known as "Life and Work" and "Faith and Order" began to find a certain amount of overlapping which was wasteful of time and effort. At their separate sessions in 1936 the Universal Christian Council for Life and Work, and the Continuation Committee of the World Conference on Faith and Order, resolved to appoint a committee to review the growth of co-operation since the Stockholm and Lausanne conferences, and to report to their Oxford and Edinburgh world conferences to be held in 1937.

This committee of thirty-five people representing the two movements and various churches and international organizations recommended the foundation of a world council of churches. Fourteen representatives, deputed to revise and complete the scheme, consulted with church representatives at Utrecht in 1938 where the "basis" and "authority" and a draft constitution of the envisaged World Council of Churches was settled, a plan for interim arrangements drawn up and a provisional committee appointed to function until the projected World Council could come into being. The constitution was sent out with an explanatory memorandum by Archbishop Temple and a letter of invitation was addressed to those churches which had been invited to the Oxford and Edinburgh conferences with some additions. At the end of the year the International Missionary Council (of which the Army is also a member) held its memorable world conference at Tambaram, Madras, which, among other things, authorized the committee to carry forward negotiations with a view to establishing mutually helpful relationships between the I.M.C. and the planned W.C.C. (This year at New Delhi the two movements will merge after many years of fruitful co-operation!)

World Assembly Commenced

The date for the First Assembly of the World Council of Churches was fixed for August 1941 but war came and the

Assembly first met in 1948 at Amsterdam. In spite of the war the number of churches had grown from 55 in 1939 to 90 in 1945 and today stands at 178. The Christian International Commission for Refugees formed in London in 1934 under the leadership of the Bishop of Chichester merged with the World Council of Churches Special Committee on Refugees and became the Ecumenical Refugee Commission.

The idea of a Department of Reconstruction had been conceived in 1942 as a means by which "all churches that can help come to the rescue of all churches which need help" and the European Central Office for Inter-Church Aid which had been established in 1922 agreed to a merger with the World Council of Churches, and this was completed by October 1945 to form the present Department of Reconstruction and Inter-Church Aid. The World Council also organized a youth department and later a Commission on International Affairs was set up.

The "basis" on which the Council was formed was that of *"a fellowship of churches which accept our Lord Jesus Christ as God and Saviour."* It was planned to carry on the work of the two world movements for "Faith and Order" and for "Life and Work"; to facilitate common action by the churches, and promote cooperation in study; to promote the growth of ecumenical consciousness and establish relations with denominational federations of world-wide scope and with other ecumenical movements; and to call world conferences on specific subjects as occasion may require.

The Council is ruled by the Assembly which was expected ordinarily to meet every five years but which, in fact, met in 1948 in Amsterdam, in 1954 in Evanston and is to meet in 1961 in Delhi. The assembly appoints the central committee which meets normally once a year and appoints its own executive committee.

After the death of Archbishop Temple the provisional committee appointed a presidium of five presidents. The secretariat is led by the General Secretary, Dr. Visser't Hooft.

4. What is the relationship of the Army to the World Council of Churches?

In an *"Officer"* article in March 1954 General Orsborn said: "We have been associated with the World Council of Churches from its very beginning. The late Commissioner A. G. Cunningham was our permanent representative on the Central Committee and ultimately became a valued member of the Executive Committee." The Army's name appeared on the list of member-churches which was published in preparation for the First Assembly of the new Council in Amsterdam in 1948, and in the workbook which has just been sent to delegates in preparation for the Third Assembly the Army is similarly listed. It sent a delegation of five to Amsterdam, of six to the Second Assembly at Evanston in 1954 and is sending nine delegates and a youth representative to New Delhi in 1961.

As Commissioner Gordon Simpson, leader of the Evanston Delegation, in introducing his report seven years ago, said: "The Army's representation at such gatherings is the logical consummation of a progressive policy of participation in inter-church activities during the leadership of General Bramwell Booth, General Edward Higgins, General Evangeline Booth, General George Carpenter and General Albert Orsborn."

In 1916 General Bramwell Booth appointed the then Colonel Charles Jeffries and Colonel A. G. Cunningham to the Council of "The Christian Crusade," a joint evangelistic effort in which representatives of all denominations in Britain participated. Later, Colonel A. G. Cunningham represented the Army at "The World Alliance for International Friendship through the Churches."

We are almost universally recognized as a religious denomination by governments and, for purposes of a national emergency—such as war service—or for convenience in designating our officers, they group us with the churches. "We are friendly with all whom Christ has named His own, and for that primary reason we do not refuse fellowship with the World Council of Churches."

5. Apart from the representative from International Headquarters, can any territory become a member?

While in overseas territories Army officers serve on many national councils of churches and inter-church councils, the constitution of the World Council of Churches itself does not make it possible for a territory to become a member direct. *To be admitted, a church must be autonomous, which is defined as meaning that it is not responsible to any other church for the conduct of its own life, including the training, ordination and maintenance of its ministry, the propagation of the Christian message, the determination of relationship with other churches and the use of funds at its disposal from whatever source.*

In this sense territories are regarded as being an integral part of The Salvation Army itself which is already a member, and not autonomous in the way that, say, the Church of England in Ghana now is. Nevertheless, being an integral part of the Army any Salvationist in any territory in the world in entitled to say that The Salvation Army to which he belongs is a member of the World Council of Churches.

6. What can the Salvationist say to those who may, through insufficient knowledge, question whether it is a good thing for the Army to be in membership with the World Council of Churches? Is there no danger that the Army's specific witness might be clouded by the appearance of a tacit approval thereby given to doctrines which differ from those we hold?

There is a sect in Britain which is at the moment losing thousands of members because it interprets "Come out from among them and be ye separate" as forbidding its members who are skippers of fishing vessels to eat at the same table as their crews, and which is prepared to excommunicate a member for being at her own sister's wedding if that wedding takes place at another church. The Salvation Army has never considered separation from the world to mean withdrawal from the society of men. Thousands of Salvationists spend all day and every day co-operating with non-Salvationists and non-believers in building ships or making shoes and serve in trade unions or employers' federations, local government or Parliament without clouding their witness, and many cooperate with us in social institutions and office work without our giving approval to their faith or lack of it. How much less could the Army neglect opportunities to cooperate with other Christians in many matters of mutual concern because they have not yet been enrolled under the flag or signed our Articles of War.

We could no more make compliance with Army teaching and method a condition of co-operation than they could require us to take the sacraments or conform in some other way before they would associate with us. The "basis" of the association is that all its members accept the Lordship of Jesus Christ, and whatever superficial differences there may be, those who are members of the Kingdom of Christ are fellow citizens of ours. Who are they to deny that we are a real and integral part of the one Church of Christ on earth? Who are we to say that they are not? On their part the initiators of the World Council of Churches have accepted the Army as a church from the beginning without departing in any way from their own principles or attempting in any way to obscure the Army's non-sacramental position, its order of ministry including its use of women for all the duties and responsibilities open to men, or any other differences.

7. But is not the non-sacramental position of the Army, for instance, even though accepted by others, likely to be a source of embarrassment, especially when members are brought together at large ecumenical gatherings?

Experience has shown this not to be so. When the matter has been mentioned it has been fully reported. The January

1958 issue of the *Ecumenical Review* published by the W.C.C., for instance, contained reports of the Oberlin Conference which studied many aspects of Faith and Order, including the place of "the table of the Lord," in Christian worship. A footnote provided by delegates of the Quakers and the Army said:

> ... We find great inspiration in the new depth of meaning which the report gives to the act of communion with our Lord. However, we wish to interpret this report in accordance with our belief in the non-necessity of the outward elements of bread and wine to mediate the living presence of Christ to the believer in the act of communion with Him.

Some Salvationists attending the Lausanne Ecumenical Youth Conference in 1960 may well have gone wondering whether the Army's non-sacramental position might in any way dampen fellowship. What they found in practice was that fellowship at every level was complete till it came to the question of the sacraments and then, far from any cleavage appearing between the Salvationists and the Quakers on the one hand and the communicants on the other, the tensions and frustrations were between those who regarded the sacrament as essential but were not allowed to kneel together at the Lord's table. Though the young people concerned pressed for arrangements which would avoid similar disappointment at the Leicester Ecumenical Youth Conference planned for 1962, it has still not been possible to find a solution and after much debating the British Council of Churches at its spring meeting could still only propose two separate communion services for Leicester. Salvationists as a matter of fact were outside these tensions, though naturally greatly disturbed to see so many earnest young people so frustrated at being denied the opportunity to make such a gesture of unity on an international inter-denominational occasion.

Quaker Position

That there is, however, deep understanding for the position of the Army and the Quakers on this subject was made plain by Dean Douglas Horton, chairman of the Faith and Order Commission of the World Council of Churches, at St. Andrews in 1960 when, on this very subject of "the breaking of the one bread," he said:

> *Those of us who use bread in the holy communion, leavened or unleavened, take for granted the need for unity at the Holy Table and may be a little perplexed when we look at the Friends' meeting and see no Holy Table at all ... but to believe that they have given up communion with Christ and one another is to misunderstand their manner of life. It is the bread of the spirit which they eat under many forms ... all of us will admit that unless (Christ's everlasting) mercy is appropriated in the rite the wheaten bread is chaff; but which of us can find it in his heart to believe that those who take their communion in an utterly non-ritual form do not eat the bread of heaven? ... "I am the bread of life," said our Lord—and that is the only bread we want, whatever the forms connected with the taking of it may be.*

8. At its meeting in 1960 the Commission on Faith and Order of the World Council of Churches spoke of "a fully committed fellowship with one another through one baptism into Him ... ." How does the Army's non-use of baptism fit into this picture of unity?

Sprinkling, or total immersion, the christening of infants, or believers baptism by water is used by many as a ceremony of initiation into the Christian Church. But those who use water at this service of introduction use it as a symbol and hold that what is vital is that there is a point at which the believer enters into living membership of the Church of Christ. Water baptism is simply a symbol, and not the medium of salvation— "it, being a sign, must answer the things signified," as the First Confession of 1646 put it for Baptists. Professor H.H. Rowley, a well-known Baptist, recently wrote: "The symbol is worthless without that which it symbolizes."

What the church understands by the phrase, *one baptism,* was recently defined as signifying the initial recognition of a member of the Church of Jesus Christ. Speaking to this point in the meeting to which our question has in fact referred, Dean Douglas Horton said, "If you confine our definition of baptism to baptism by water, then indeed it cannot be regarded as one of the essentials of unity held by all our members, but if you allow baptism to mean essentially the adoption of a person into the bosom of Christ's Church … then it seems to me that … baptism becomes a foundation stone of the city all of us are seeking.… The phrase, *one baptism,* is a rhetorically succinct way of describing a mode of Christian adoption whereby whether one is baptized in the Anglican way, or the Baptist way, or the Campbellite way … the Quaker way, or any other, he finds himself recognized as being in the one Church … that there should be for all the forms, the one outcome, entrance into Christ's Church, is part of our common vision of unity."

It is on this basis, no doubt, that the new and beautifully produced World Council of Churches booklet, "Ye are baptized," includes in its descriptions a statement of the Army's position and presents a photograph of a Salvation Army enrollment beneath the flag among other photographs of the moment of public admission to membership of the Church of Christ. Here is a real understanding of the true meaning of Christian initiation and a definition that causes no embarrassment for us or our friends.

9. Since the Founder decided against union with the Church of England nearly eighty years ago, is there not a danger that membership of the World Council of Churches might be regarded as the first step toward a time when the Army's distinctive witness might become lost in a somewhat indeterminate world church?

The World Council of Churches never supposed that it had to bring about unity. The unity was there already. "The Church of Christ on earth is one," as General Bramwell Booth said, though there have been times when rivalry, competition, overlapping of effort, animosity and even persecution of Christians by one another may have given the world the opposite impression. The World Council is concerned that the essential unity that exists should become apparent to all. The Council is a means of manifesting this unity, but as Dean Horton said: "If the report had suggested in any way that our unity must take some particular form we should have had to give it up, but this it does not do."

The newly enthroned Archbishop of Canterbury, Dr. Michael Ramsey, speaking of "churchly unity," warned against the danger of isolating the concept of unity. The idea comes from John 17 (His Grace pointed out) where our Lord's prayer for the unity of His disciples is interwoven with His prayer for their sanctification and their fidelity to the truth. "Unity, truth and holiness are inseparable," Ramsey said.

All this has had to do with unity and not union. The Council cannot and must not negotiate union between the churches. It cannot speak for the churches in any way without their consent, it does not legislate for the churches—"no church need fear that its membership in the council will mean that it will be forced into organic unity with other churches," Ramsey declared.

No Union But Unity

It is interesting to observe, by the way, that, in spite of the growth of the ecumenical idea in Great Britain since 1910, not one single union of churches belonging to different confessional or denominational families has taken place in these years.

The Rev. Kenneth Slack says in his new book, *The British Churches Today:* "The modern ecumenical movement is based upon the conviction that churchmanship matters and that the loyalty we have to our own church must be taken with great seriousness. On the basis of a common commitment to Christ even before there is any doctrinal agreement we are called together to seek a visible unity. That search must be on the basis of an honest recognition of ecclesiastical differences and the treasure in differing church traditions."

Nevertheless, in days of growing insecurity, increasing secularism, lowering standards, and international instability, Christians everywhere must cherish the sense of unity with other Christians throughout the world and form a common front against the common foe. When Japan and China were at war a Chinese woman found herself in the hands of a Japanese officer and wondered where he was taking her. To her relief it turned out to be a church. "This woman is in grave danger," the officer said to the minister, "please take care of her." Then with a low bow he added, "I, too, am a Christian"—which is what unity means.

Prayer Requested

Salvationists will at this time pray more earnestly than ever for the forward march of the Church of Christ. As the letter of invitation sent out so many years ago affirmed: "Christians should never be dismayed as they face the challenge of the world looking to the Risen Christ; they find in that challenge a call to go forward in His Name."

14

The Salvation Army and the World Council of Churches

by Clarence D. Wiseman

Notes of a lecture to the cadets,
Toronto College For Officers' Training, 1970

IN the early part of the 20th Century, new trends appeared in those areas of the Christian Church usually called Protestants, heirs of the 16th Century Reformation. These trends revealed themselves in three Movements, which since have been merged to form the present World Council of Churches:

The International Missionary Council—formed in 1921. It grew out of a World Missionary Conference held in Edinburgh in 1910. Through its membership in various affiliated groups the Army had indirect relations with the I. M. C.

The Life and Work Movement. This was launched in Sweden in 1925 by representatives of the main European and American Protestant Churches. The Movement had to do with the churches' relation with and messages to the social and political life of the people. It was rooted in every-day affairs—*life* and *work* as the title suggests.

The Faith and Order Movement. This Movement emerged about 1927 and was concerned with theological issues, especially those that served to separate the churches, such delicate questions as doctrine, liturgy, worship.

In 1937 it was proposed that "Life and Work" and "Faith and Order" should unite, and a constitution of the proposed World Council of Churches was submitted to the churches for consideration. However, World War II intervened, and the First Assembly of the World Council of Churches could not be held until 1948 when Church representatives meeting in Amsterdam, formed the Council. Commissioner A. G. Cunningham represented the Army, which became a charter member.

Several Important Questions Relative to the Army's Membership in the W.C.C. Are Raised in Different Parts of the World:

1. Is the *Statement of Faith* to which members must subscribe, adequate?
   a. From beginning it was recognized that churches had a common faith in one Lord and Saviour Jesus Christ. Hence first basis was a simple declaration of this truth: **The World Council of Churches is a fellowship of churches which accept our Lord Jesus Christ as God and Saviour.**
   b. As time went on, it became clear that this was not enough. Hence an extended basis was adopted at the Third Assembly held in New Delhi in 1961:
   The World Council of Churches is a fellowship of churches which confess the Lord Jesus Christ as God and Saviour according to the Scriptures and therefore seek to fulfil together their common calling to the glory of the one God, Father, Son and Holy Spirit.

114

This basis was never intended to be a creed or confession, but simply the affirmation of a central rallying point of doctrine for the churches.

2. Will the Army be drawn into union with churches against its will?

   a. We must distinguish between "union" which refers to organization and "unity" which has to do with things of the Spirit. Dr. Visser't Hooft once said: "The New Testament makes clear that unity in Christ does not mean uniformity and centralization."

   b. The constitution of the W.C.C. prevents that body from trying to compel any member into union with another member. It was confirmed at New Delhi that:

      (i) The W.C.C. cannot attempt to violate the autonomy of any member church;

      (ii) Neither can it make pronouncements on unity that contravene the recognized doctrines of member churches;

      (iii) Neither will it seek to impose any one conception of unity.

   c. The W.C.C. is not, and cannot become, a Church. A statement on this was made by the Central Committee in 1963: ***The World Council of Churches is neither the Church, nor a church, nor the super church. The W.C.C. is by its very nature the servant of the churches.***

   d. Nowhere in the Army world is the Army in negotiation with any other church body with union in mind; such negotiations would require the consent of the General, and there is no likelihood of such an event happening in the foreseeable future.

3. Should The Salvation Army have fellowship with other churches in the W.C.C. that do not see eye to eye with us on doctrinal matters?

a. It is important that we give attention to the full teaching of the Bible when replying to such a question, and not rest our decision on isolated passages.

b. We have no right to separate from those who differ doctrinally, but who truly own Jesus Christ as Lord and Saviour. Nor have we any right to deny them fellowship.

In Mark 9:39 the Lord says, "Forbid him not, for there is no man which shall do a mighty work in my name that will be able soon after to speak evil of me, for he that is not against us is for us."

c. When the Bible says, "Come out from among them and be ye separate" (2 Cor. 6:17), what does it mean? It doesn't mean, "Separate yourself from all fellowship with this church or that church because they have some doctrines that differ from yours." For the Corinthians it meant, "Come out from the temples of Venus and Jupiter with their heathen worship and sensual practices; separate yourselves from the evil of devil worship."

The Bible tells us to be separate from the world, from pagan ceremony, and from devil worship; but when it comes to separation from other Christians, the only biblical basis is on moral grounds. We are to be separate from Christians who are living immoral and unworthy lives, so that the world may know that the Christian Church is called to a higher standard.

d. Is there any justification for separation on doctrinal grounds? In 2 John 7 and 10 we read, "For many deceivers are entered into the world who confess not that Jesus Christ is come in the flesh ... if there come any unto you and bring not this doctrine, receive him not into your home...." The false teacher is the one who denies Jesus Christ. From such we are to separate ourselves.

e. It is good that God has not made us judges of other

people. We are not to pull out the tares, "Lest", as Jesus reminds us, "in gathering the tares you root up the wheat along with them." To us this means, "Don't consign this man to hell because he doesn't believe exactly as you believe. He may well be one of the Lord's sheep who has had too little teaching or too much criticism. Deal with him in love, and leave judgment to God."

f. Some people say, "But we must protect the faith." Does the Word of God need our protection? Surely this is the work of the Holy Spirit. We are called, not to protect the Word of God, but to demonstrate the Word of God, as Paul reminds us in Phil. 2:13-16.

4. Some suggest that the W.C.C. is leading its members toward union with the Roman Catholic Church.

It is true that a committee of the W.C.C. is engaged in conversations with a committee of the Roman Catholic Church. One must remember that since Pope John, the Roman Catholic Church has adopted a more open and friendly attitude to other churches than prevailed previously. However, as indicated earlier, the W.C.C. cannot lead any member church into closer relations with any other church against its will. Furthermore, while Salvationists will always live on friendly terms with fellow-Christians of the Roman Catholic Communion, we cannot ignore the deep doctrinal differences that exist, especially as related to such questions as Papal Infallibility, Mariolatry and Transubstantiation.

In conclusion: Catherine Booth, Mother of The Salvation Army, said to Salvationists in 1883: "It is not your business to go and find fault with other people. Rejoice in all the good done, by whomsoever it is done. Be glad whenever you find a good man or a good woman at work for God, and for the salvation of the people. Never try to find a hole in their coat, or pull them to pieces. Mind your own business which is seeking and saving the lost."

The Salvation Army must retain its own identity as a Movement within the "Body of Christ." Many Salvationists are unaware of the fact that as early as 1882 the Church of England set up a committee to consider the possibility of "alliance with The Salvation Army." General William Booth, in response to these enquiries, said he was willing "for the two organizations to run side by side like two rivers, with bridges thrown across, over which the members could mutually pass and repass" ... but he went on to emphasize that the Army could never submit to the authority of the Church (which was the State Church of England), nor could it abandon its central position concerning the primacy of conversion, nor give up its firmly established conviction that the catholic sacraments were not necessary to salvation.

In *Echoes and Memories,* Bramwell Booth said, "Of this, the Great Church of the Living God, we claim and ever have claimed, that we of The Salvation Army are an integral part and element—a living, fruit-bearing branch of the true Vine."

15

One in Charity

by Arnold Brown

From *The Gate and the Light*, published by
Bookwright Publications, Toronto, 1984. Used
by permission.

MY wife and I were again in charming Leysin, resting for a
few days amid the beauty of the Swiss Alps, when a
telephone call from London, England, disturbed more than
our furlough. The outcome of this conversation with the Chief
of the Staff— "suspension from the World Council of
Churches pending dialogue"—was to stir the minds and
feelings of Salvationists around the world. It was also to
engender enormous media coverage and to be the subject
of impassioned debates in the church councils of the world.
The Chief conveyed the news that the fires of uneasiness,
smouldering since 1970 concerning the direction of the
World Council of Churches' policies, had been fuelled by a
grant of $85,000 to the Rhodesian Patriotic Front led by
Joshua Nkomo.

It was a particularly bitter period in the Rhodesian deba-
cle, and, immediately following the announcement, perplexed Salvationists and others were demanding to know if
the grant meant the espousal of violence by the World
Council and whether the Army, by the law of association, was
party to it. Donors flooded the various headquarters with

letters and telephone calls asking if monies given to the Army had found their way, via the W.C.C., to this allocation. I knew that no contribution had been made by the Army to the Program to Combat Racism. I also knew that no movement could more visibly have demonstrated its total commitment in a practical way to all in need, of whatever color or culture.

It would be unfair to make a sweeping denunciation of the council's grant aid program. Many allocations were to worthy causes and deserved commendation. But there were aspects of this latest, and similarly placed grants since 1971, that created criticism. The grant was ostensibly for relief in food, clothing and medicine, but there was no guarantee that the funds would be so applied. Even if they were, it meant that such aid would be releasing other monies with which the war effort could be pursued. Simple logic suggested that one way or the other the grant could subsidize the escalating violence. I wanted it made clear that the Army was not protesting against the aims of the Patriotic Front. Our reaction was certainly not anti-liberation nor pro-white. That the W.C.C. should be pleading for disarmament and peace and, at the same time, be supporting users of armed terrorism was, to our way of thinking, inconsistent. The grant appeared to be so specifically placed as to indicate a political inclination on the part of the council, in contrast to The Salvation Army's traditional non-political basis.

For ninety years the Army had been part of Rhodesia's national life, with strong participation in the fields of education and health care. Its officers knew that not only Nkomo's followers, but numbers of black Rhodesians holding quite different political aspirations, were in dire need due to the internecine struggle that had disastrously interfered with the production and availability of life's necessities. Grants made equally to all factions at this particularly tense moment would, it was felt, have reflected the concern of the churches for the total problem, and would have eliminated any undesirable element of partiality from which political conclusions could rightly or wrongly be drawn. The grant was also given without any requirement of accountability. To my mind this was unwise. The giving of funds "on trust as an evidence of total commitment" seemed exceedingly naive. Our own indigenous leaders were aware of widespread indiscipline in the handling of monies and were doing their best to develop a high degree of fiscal responsibility. Generosity of this kind, however highly motivated, splintered respect for those standards of accountability which were being established with much difficulty.

A further point was the disregard of the presence in Rhodesia of the council's member churches and their ability to be the purveyors of relief. Their long and intimate knowledge of both the people and their needs, and, for certain of them, proven experience in meeting calamitous situations, apparently counted for little. To have used them, and among them The Salvation Army, would have enhanced the churches' relationships with the people. By-passing them created the impression that the council was uncertain about the expertise of their own member churches, but were confident of the Patriotic Front's management capabilities.

It is now history that the Patriotic Front did not come to power. If the grant had been made on the basis of the rightness of this particular faction's cause above all others then politically it failed. One can only hope that the grant eased the severe lot of some whose husbands and fathers were caught up, many of them unwittingly and unwillingly, in a conflict for power about which they knew little or nothing.

It is necessary in the interests of accuracy, and for the record, to state that the grants by the Program to Combat Racism were not the sole or chief cause for the rift between the Army and the Council, a rift that had widened with the passing years, and particularly during the Seventies. The growing gap was regrettable since the Army was involved with the World Council of Churches from its inception. In 1910 a World Missionary Conference held in Edinburgh discussed European and American responsibility for spreading the Gospel and this led, in 1921, to the formation of the International Missionary Council. Four years later, delegates from various Christian denominations met in Stockholm and discussed the application of Christian principles to world problems. The result was the creation of the Universal Christian Council on Life and Work. In 1927 a World Conference on Faith and Order was held to deal with doctrinal divisions between denominations. The two last-mentioned conferences met respectively in Oxford and Edinburgh in the same year, 1937, to agree on a plan for union. Only a year later a group of representatives met in Utrecht and laid plans for an envisaged World Council of Churches. It existed in embryo for the next decade sponsoring inter-church relationships and rendering worthy service during the years of the Second World War.

The World Council of Churches inaugural assembly was held in Amsterdam in August 1948, with 146 member churches representing forty-six countries, of which forty-two churches were from the Third World. Included in the church representation were ten "black" churches. All member churches were to be autonomous, and a minimum membership of 25,000 was required for admission to the council. Twenty years later, at the Uppsala Assembly, one hundred and three Third World churches, including forty-one African, were registered, reflecting the upsurge of indigenous denominations. Today there are some three hundred member churches representing one hundred countries.

Prior to the First Assembly in 1948, the advisory council to the General brought into being as the result of a pledge given by General Albert Orsborn to his electors in 1946, had, as one of its first matters for consideration, "The Salvation Army's relation with national and world councils of churches." The General, in his request for a recommendation, said, "I have my own views, but I do not wish to impose them on others," and then went on to express them in a six-page memorandum. The document concluded with: "I do not wish my period of leadership to be associated with the gravitation of The Salvation Army nearer to church life in faith and order," a view evidently not generally held seeing the advisory council responded with an eight-page statement summarized in one sentence: "The advisory council has no hesitation in recommending that The Salvation Army continues its membership of the World Council of Churches." The General then gave his decision concerning Salvation Army representation at the First Assembly in grudging terms: "It occurs to me to wonder why we should participate in the assembly ... but the majority of our leaders think that we should be represented and therefore I have told the Chief to arrange it."

As defined by its constitution the World Council "is a fellowship of churches which confess the Lord Jesus Christ as God and Saviour according to the Scriptures and therefore seek to fulfil together their common calling to the glory of the one God, Father, Son and Holy Spirit." To this theological basis for admission The Salvation Army could commit itself unreservedly, and sent representatives to all meetings of the highest authoritative body of the council—the assembly; in 1948 at Amsterdam, Netherlands; in 1954 at Evanston, USA; in 1961 at New Delhi, India; in 1968 at Uppsala, Sweden and in 1975 at Nairobi, Kenya. A Salvation Army leader, Commissioner A. G. Cunningham, was elected to the first central committee of the World Council thus confirming the Army's membership as a constituent "church" from the beginning. He was succeeded by a number of outstanding leaders including Commissioners Frank Evans, Clarence D. Wiseman, Herbert Westcott, Harry Williams and Victor Keanie, and Colonel Ernest N. Denham.

Only weeks before the controversial grant was made to the Patriotic Front two Salvation Army girls, one a Lieutenant, Diane Thompson, of London, England, and the other a lay worker from Northern Ireland, Sharon Swindells, had been murdered by freedom fighters at the Usher Secondary School where they were serving. The killing appalled Salvationists. Some were angered. They, like many non-Salvationists, felt that the death of the two young women was a clear signal that violence had gone mad and that any control of men under arms was mythical. Not once, however, was this happening mentioned officially in our dealings with the World Council of Churches. We did not want our protest over the grant to be in any way regarded as an emotional reaction to the death of the girl Salvationists. Other missions suffered more severely than the Army in the loss of expatriate workers' lives and, as grievous as was the loss of the two splendid women, it was well-known to me and my associates that the lives of many other Salvationists had been taken. That they were black did not make their death any less a loss to the Army. At war's end, when the rolls were cursorily checked, our leaders in the renamed Zimbabwe informed me that, sadly, somewhere between four and six thousand of our people had lost their lives in the struggle.

The 1978 grant, however, seemed to be "the last straw." Protests concerning earlier grants registered by the Army's representatives serving as members of the central committee had merited little response. What little acknowledgement there had been was patronizing. More importantly, through the decade the council's tendency to politically-inclined action appeared increasingly to override that evangelical thrust which the Army and other church bodies had longed for as a result of the closer inter-involvement of the denominations. A spreading acceptance of "liberation theology" as being primarily a Scriptural mandate to social action in the temporal sphere, and in certain circumstances justifying violence, was viewed with profound misgiving. Christ's testimony, "The Spirit of the Lord is upon me, because He hath anointed me ... to preach deliverance to the captives ... to set at liberty them that are bruised" (Luke 4: 18), for us meant the possibility of spiritual liberation for the sin-bound individual through Christ's sacrifice on the Cross. It appeared as if the word of Dr. Headlam, Bishop of Gloucester, at the Malvern Conference in 1924, was prophetic. He foresaw that a World Council would be "continually involved in political matters and controversy, and largely influenced by the passion for identifying Christianity with socialism."

In proposing to the Chief "suspension pending dialogue," I asked for the opinion not only of Commissioner Williams, our current member of the central committee, but also of the advisory council to the General, before such a step were taken. All felt that "dialogue" was important, and that the step of "suspension" was the only way by which this could be hastened. Commissioner Williams' views were particularly important. He had been nominated by General Wiseman during a commissioners' conference at Sunbury Court in 1975 to fill the vacancy on the central committee (left open since the retirement of Commissioner Westcott) in view of the imminent Assembly at Nairobi. Some felt that this particular assembly could be a "watershed," and that the direction of its flow, theologically and practically, would determine whether or not the Army should remain in membership.

Before leaving Leysin, I authorized the Chief to give the decision to the World Council and to Army leaders. By the time my wife and I reached London the following weekend the whole world, it seemed, also knew of the decision. The "dialogue" aspect, generally speaking, was ignored by the media. The "suspension" element was headlined as "Salvation Army Quits World Council of Churches." Perhaps I had been ingenuous in thinking that the matter was a private one between a member and the body with which the member was affiliated. Seated at lunch almost two years later beside the venerable ecumenist, Dr. Visser't Hooft, he likened our suspension to a family disagreement. "All families have them," he said, "but the family doesn't break up because of

125

them." I admit to having thought of our suspension, and the need for conversation, as purely a family affair, but privacy within the house of *Oikumene* was not to be. The world took sides, and I found myself to be a tennis net above which balls flew with speed and force and, into which, not infrequently, volleys landed rather painfully.

Dr. Philip Potter, general secretary of the council, responded quickly by coming from Geneva to see me at International Headquarters. It was our first meeting and it confirmed all I had heard of his many gifts. Personable and articulate, he had my immediate respect. The reason for any misunderstandings was defined by him as due to lack of communication. We, perhaps, had not fully understood the council's motives and philosophy, while he and his colleagues, he admitted somewhat ruefully, had taken the Army very much for granted, though tremendously appreciating its work and witness. In this discussion I expressed the deep concern of many Salvationists at what appeared to be the politicization of the council. I asked if the council, by involving itself in certain sensitive national issues was not subscribing to a lesser function rather than honouring its greater mission, the evangelization of the world by the power of the Gospel? The views of Dr. Potter and myself on the "revolutionary" character of Jesus hardly coincided.

Dr. Potter proposed a meeting of members of his secretariat with Army leaders, and this was set for the 12th of December at International Headquarters in London. The date was easy to remember, it would be the eve of my 65th birthday. The group met in the board room of the Advisory Council to the General, a room dominated by a large and excellent portrait of General Bramwell Booth, cloak about his shoulders and pince-nez in hand. Supporting me were the Chief of the Staff and several commissioners. The Geneva delegation was led by the moderator, Archbishop Ted Scott, of Canada, who suggested that he and I should jointly preside. If differing views were to be expressed the accent would be the same!

The day and the discussions left me with a mosaic of impressions—the compelling quality of Christian fraternity; the almost fanatical commitment to the cause of ecumenism of certain of our visitors; the solidarity of Salvationists in their less-articulated but unequivocal allegiance to evangelism; my own nervousness when frequently required to advance a proposition or sum up for our side; and not least the inspiration I received from the choicely-phrased prayers offered by the archbishop. He, I felt, was uncomfortable in confrontation; he is more pastor than prefect.

To the theological basis of membership in the council, adopted in 1948 at the Amsterdam Assembly, a later, additional statement implied that the World Council of Churches was to be a "Eucharistic Fellowship." For the Army, as a non-sacramental body, this could mean exclusion, certainly so if organic union became a reality. The archbishop took pains to explain that the phrase should be interpreted in its widest sense as "a fellowship of thanksgiving," which he insisted, could not debar the Army and its joyous witness. The elucidation was offered helpfully, but it remained clear that for a vast number of leading churchmen the Eucharist meant the celebration of a rite not practiced by Salvationists, a fact which, in their thinking, determined the "church-ness," or otherwise, of a religious group.

The fact that printed references to the Army's membership in the Council's publications had relegated us as an international movement to a London, England, group, was something that could immediately be corrected. This point was quicky and good-naturedly despatched. Discussion concerning the Program to Combat Racism was less easily dealt with, and there was an animated exchange when certain commissioners wanted to know what was, in the mind of the Council, its true magnetic North in respect of global evangelism and world ministry. Regrettably, the day did not finish as it began. In the final half-hour, restraint somehow evaporated. In astringent and, at one point, emotional terms, the general secretary, and the one woman member of the council's delegation, gave the Army a "woodshed lecture." The mature adult sought to instruct the wilful child. Perhaps the dispensers felt they could not be true to themselves without doing so, but it was an exercise that put a sting into the tail of the conference. I went home with my own emotions in turmoil.

I had informed the conference that no final decision concerning the Army's future relationship with the Council could be given until after the International Conference of Leaders scheduled to be held in Toronto in September 1979, and, apart from providing Army leaders with details of the meeting and gaining their reaction, the matter was dormant through the intervening months. In Toronto, the debate was serious and frequently intense. All knew that a decision would have to be reached; we could not stay "in suspension" indefinitely, and I had indicated that I did not want to enter retirement with this piece of business unfinished. There were various views and an early consensus was obviously impossible. Delegates were asked on returning to their appointments to review the whole subject in the light of the latest information given them. The conference then asked that a letter be sent to Dr. Potter, and on behalf of the delegates I signed the following prepared message:

1st October, 1979

Dear Dr. Potter,

I promised that after free consultation with the commissioners of The Salvation Army in September, 1979, I would give you an answer of the matter of The Salvation Army's membership of the World Council of Churches.

When the subject was reviewed during an international conference of leaders it became evident that there were several deeper aspects of the relationship which required that further kind of examination which the duration of our conference did not allow. Our leaders did feel it would be helpful if I restated the priorities for which our world-wide movement is known:

(1) Evangelism.

(2) Concern for the poor and oppressed without distinction of race or creed and which is not partisan in terms of support for any specific party.

(3) A history of support for socio-political changes which eschew violence.

(4) A branch of the Church which does not practice the rites of Baptism and the Eucharist, and commissions women equally with men, admitting them to all offices.

Committed as we are to these priorities, it is felt that there has been a gradual shift in the World Council of Churches' own emphasis which often makes us appear out of step.

In view of the recommendation made at the central committee of the World Council of Churches at Kingston in January, 1979, to institute consultations with the churches on the administration of the Special Fund to Combat Racism, deferring decision until the next meeting of the central committee. I would express the hope that the executive committee will permit the status quo *to continue until that date. During this period we will be able to conduct the further examination of our relationship referred to above.*

It will be for you to state whether our representative would be welcome at the next central meeting and at any appropriate consultations before that.

In the Name of Christ the conference sends, through you, its greetings to all the churches, with the prayer that the Holy Spirit will continue to enlarge and prosper their mission and ministry.

Yours sincerely,
(Sgd.) Arnold Brown, General

As the months went by, the returns came in, but many were inconclusively couched. Finally, a simple questionnaire offered three courses of action for which "yes" or "no" answers were required. Few wanted total severance. The majority wanted a form of relationship which preserved a spiritual unity with all member churches of the council but which unshackled the Army from the policy decisions of the executive and central committees.

By the time we were ready to submit our request for a

change to fraternal status, Dr. Potter had gone on a sabbatical. His deputy, however, invited us to come to Geneva immediately following the general secretary's return, and on June 3, 1981, we were warmly received in conference, Archbishop Scott acting as chairman. One could only admire the persistence of the chairman, the general secretary and others who represented the World Council in seeking to retain the Army's full membership. I explained that the best possible consensus of Salvation Army views had been secured, and that our delegation, with the recommendation of the Advisory Council to the General, had come not to debate the issue but to conclude it. I can only describe the atmosphere as one of affable emptiness in which all arguments had been neutralized. Only one outburst momentarily altered the ambience. A recent appointee of the Council charged us with "deliberately amputating the Body of Christ." The statement was extravagant, and I assured our friend that we had no desire to "amputate" ourselves from any unity of the spirit or in any way to dismember the body of Christian kinship.

Under the council's constitution the change of status we sought could not be effected without first withdrawing from full membership and afterwards applying for fraternal relationship. The technical procedure was recognized but, sensing what the media treatment would be, I had hoped that "withdrawal" would be less emphasized than a "change of relationship." This was not to be. The chairman then proposed that each delegation should separately have a period of reflection and prayer. When we regrouped, the Council's delegation appeared to have given up any attempt to retain our membership and manifested only a desire to work out the mechanics of the change as efficiently and cooperatively as possible. It was agreed that our letter requesting a change of status should be presented at the next meeting of the central committee due to be held in Dresden, East Germany and, on the basis of the committee's decision, an agreed news release would be issued jointly.

I sent the following letter from London:

31st July, 1981

Dear Dr. Potter,

Members of the Salvation Army delegation which you and your colleagues received so cordially in Geneva on June 3rd have given further prayerful reflection to those helpful deliberations, and the subject of The Salvation Army's relationship with the World Council of Churches has also had the renewed attention of the Advisory Council to the General.

The feeling is that those who carry the chief responsibility for the World Council of Churches have been exceedingly patient not only in correspondence but also in allowing us ample time to study those aspects of the relationship that have troubled many Salvationists. We are aware that to be "in suspension pending dialogue" was, under the World Council of Churches' constitution, an unrecognized status and, because of this, your tolerance has been all the more appreciated.

The time has come, however, to resolve the situation, and we therefore ask for an adjustment in the relationship that presently exists. The Salvation Army wishes to move from full membership to fraternal status under the provision in the Constitution (Section VI, 1, and Section XII of the Rules).

In making this request we are acting on the best consensus we can gain, based on the most careful polling of our world-wide leadership, and via the processes explained in detail during our deliberations in Geneva on June 3rd.

The reasons for this submission have been shared with you, and at length. In summary, they revolve around the fact of The Salvation Army's internationality which itself implies diversity of views concerning our relationship. The preservation of that internationality, by the very nature of our movement, is vital to us, and, we feel, to those whom we serve.

To lose any spiritual fellowship with the World Council of Churches would be for us as undesirable and painful as it would be if we were to sever the happy relationship we enjoy with local, regional and national councils of churches around the world, as well as with the various communions and denominations whose witness and work for Christ we prayerfully uphold and in which, in our unique way, we share.

There are unquestionably aspects of the World Council of Churches' activity which demand our full support, e.g., the Commission on Evangelism, the Commission on Faith and Order, CICARWS, and CMC. We would certainly wish to demonstrate such support in *more positive and practical ways. Our gravamen has to do with the issuance by the World Council of Churches of statements, the developing of policies and the carrying out of actions which we regard as political, and which, as such endanger the non-political nature of the Army, the preservation of which is basic to the Movement's effectiveness in a number of countries. Refusal to identify with political factions, as distinct from deep social concern for the needy people of all lands regardless of creed, colour or political persuasion, has been the essence of the Army's life and endeavour from its very beginning. Indeed, we see clearly that any such political identification would inevitably cut us off the large numbers of those very people we seek to succour. The Salvation Army's foundation belief is that the only real hope for the transformation of society lies in personal salvation through faith in the redemptive grace of Christ.*

This submission comes to you in the prayful hope that all who will be related to its consideration can accept that it is motivated only by a desire, on the one hand, to remain in the most harmonious relationship with the World Council of Churches that our position will allow, and, on the other hand, to follow a course which appears to us, after relentless heartsearching and long and prayerful study, the proper one at this particular time.

No-one knows what the future may bring. Should the day come when circumstances encourage The Salvation Army to leave fraternal status and seek full membership, I hope that our readiness to apply would be matched by the World Council of Churches' understanding.

Our constant prayer is that for you and all who share your immense responsibilities there may continue to be granted "the wisdom that cometh from above."

With warmest personal greetings and every good wish. May Divine grace be yours in overflowing measure.

Yours sincerely,
(Sgd.) Arnold Brown
General

In acknowledgement, the central committee wrote as follows:

Dear General Brown,

The central committee of the WCC received with deep regret the news of The Salvation Army's decision to resign its membership of the World Council of Churches. In your letter of 31 July, 1981, you express the desire to remain in the most harmonious possible relationship with the WCC. The committee accepts your resignation and accedes to your request for fraternal status as a world confessional body. Formally, in terms of our constitution, this means that you may be invited to send non-voting representatives to our meetings in such numbers as the central committee shall determine.

As a founding member of the WCC, The Salvation Army has belonged since 1948 to the worldwide fellowship of churches which "confess the Lord Jesus Christ as God and Saviour according to the Scriptures and therefore seek to fulfil their common calling to the glory of the one God, Father, Son and Holy Spirit." This basis of membership is open to the variety of emphases and gifts that different members bring to the total fellowship. Expression of this variety is ensured by the WCC's constitution. The central committee regrets that The Salvation Army feels that, as a member of our fellowship, it compromises its special emphasis on personal salvation through Christ as "the only real hope for the transformation of society."

In explaining the reason for your resignation of membership, you refer to statements, policies and actions of the WCC with which you take issue. Yet it has been clear from the earliest years of the council's life that no member is bound by any action of the whole council. To quote from the WCC central committee statement in 1950: "Membership in the council does not in any sense mean that the churches belong to a body which can make decisions for them. Each church retains the constitutional right to ratify or to reject utterances or actions of the council."

You describe in your letter that you have agonized over this decision since 1978 when you first suspended membership. The central committee appreciates the difficulties you found, but wishes it had been possible for you to continue the dialogue on the issues you had raised.

We feel compelled to disagree with the contrast you draw between the so-called political nature of the action of the World Council of Churches and your own claim to have a non-political stance. From its inception the World Council of Churches has always acted from the deep conviction that the imperatives of the Christian gospel affect all realms of life. Indeed, one of the constitutional functions of the council is to promote "one human family in justice and peace."

We welcome the continuing support you express in your letter for large areas of the council's work, especially world mission and evangelism, faith and order, inter-church aid and the Christian medical commission. But these programmes are inextricably bound up with all the policies of the council in all areas of its work, including the programme to combat racism, over which you have had particular difficulty.

We are aware from our conversations with you, that the World Council's search for "full eucharistic fellowship" poses problems for you as a non-sacramental movement.. We can only reiterate the assurances we have given you that this phrase is not a part of the basis for membership and therefore does not exclude you from our fellowship.

You express the hope that should the day come when The Salvation Army re-applies for membership, the World Council would meet you with understanding. We can assure you of our willingness to do so.

Meanwhile, we shall maintain cooperative working relationship at the international level, and we share your hope that at local, national and regional levels the ecumenical relationship which The Salvation Army enjoys will continue to grow.

We greet you in the Name of our Lord and Saviour Jesus Christ. On behalf of the central committee,

Edward W. Scott, Moderator
Philip A. Potter, General Secretary

Our submission was presented during the Dresden meeting and the change was agreed with accompanying expressions of regret. Something, however, went awry with the plan for a bilaterally-agreed news release. The World Council prepared its own release, embargoed until noon the following Monday; but, on the previous Sunday evening, newspapers in the Netherlands were already informing our leaders of the Army's "withdrawal" and asking for comment. When the telexed text of the release reached International Headquarters we cabled immediately asking for a revision of the heading which was worded negatively, emphasizing "withdrawal." But it was too late for change. The damage was done. Media comment, in avalanche volume, generally stressed "withdrawal," and all too many reports invested the events leading to the decision with a bitterness that existed only in the journalist's imagination.

I did not want the Army's offer of help in those areas of work on which the council and the Army saw eye to eye to be thought of as a polite, empty gesture. The offer had been made in good faith, and I was prepared to send suitable officers to the Council's staff and meet their subsistence. I felt that I should emphasize this, and accordingly wrote to the archbishop and general secretary the following letter which concluded the exchange of correspondence:

Dear friends:

Though you were kind enough to telex the contents of the central committee's letter of decision, the letter itself has now come safely to hand and, in order that the file may be left in a tidy condition for my successor and the future, I acknowledge with thanks its receipt.

It was our hope that our request for fraternal status would engender minimum media comment. Unfortunately, we felt that media stress fell more on the aspect of "withdrawal" and less on the desire of the Army to maintain a helpful relationship.

We would wish, however, to emphasize that the offers of support made during our Geneva discussions reflected our desire to be involved in those areas of Christian work and witness to which we are equally committed. I am hopeful that Commissioner Keanie will have opportunity to discuss possible ways and means with those of your officers with whom you might wish him to confer.

We are grateful for every expression and gesture of Christian fellowship you have extended to us. We have the feeling that wearers of Salvation Army uniform will always be welcome at your headquarters in Geneva, and we appreciate this. Equally, the doors of our International Headquarters will be wide open to any associated with the World Council of Churches who can visit us.

With both official and warmest personal greetings. May God continue abundantly to bless and be with you.

> *Yours sincerely,*
> *(Sgd.) Arnold Brown*
> *General*

The Army's decision, when understood, was widely supported. Only in Zimbabwe was there any kind of unhappy reaction. That, I felt, came about because the explanatory material provided to each command had not yet reached the small group of well-meaning but uninformed Salvationists who made a public protest outside our headquarters in Salisbury (now Harare). Fear that the Army's decision would forestall any further, badly-needed grants appeared to be the basis of the protest, a fear that was soon allayed by the receipt of a grant of $100,000 from the World Council for relief purposes, the money being drawn from sources other than the Program to Combat Racism Fund. The demonstation was brief, but long enough for the news cameras to film the "Down with Brown" placards. The chief participants were invited to join in discussion and a climate of understanding was soon created. Shortly afterwards the territorial commander reported that "the Army in Zimbabwe is in good health."

On reflection I see the episode of the Army's relationship to the World Council of Churches as a two-dimensional experience. One had to do with my official involvement, beginning in 1970 while Chief of the Staff, and coming to a climax in my final month as international leader. It was an organization-to-organization dimension—two international, multi-national bodies seeking to learn each other's place and function; the one, eucharistic, influential, status-conscious and somewhat monolithic. The other, non-sacramental and attempting to unite in one discipline a variety of races and views; perhaps the only truly international member of the World Council's growing family.

The other dimension was personal. I found myself dealing with individuals rather than an organization; persons for whom I developed high respect and warm regard. Through the long months of negotiation and mounting strain I came to see them as "apostles of unity" who, like myself, were not without an occasional "thorn in the flesh." What is here recorded will, I am certain, convince the most skeptical that we were, at the least, "... one in charity."

16

The Salvationist and Worship

by William Wilson

From a series entitled "Ecclesiology" in
Horizons, published by The Salvation Army,
Toronto, 1985. Used by permission.

IF worship is, as Archbishop William Temple taught, "the quickening of conscience by the holiness of God; the nourishment of mind by His truth; the purifying of imagination by His beauty; the opening of the heart to His love; the surrender of will to His purpose," why are we so reluctant to enter into this experience? If worship is "the most momentous, the most urgent, the most glorious action that can take place in human life" according to Karl Barth, why are so many so bored by it? If it is the consummation of life, why is it so often regarded as consuming time which could be better spent in a dozen different ways?

The Meaning of Worship

When worship is defined by Evelyn Underhill as "the response of the creature to the Eternal," "an acknowledgement of God as transcendent"; or by Rudolf Otto as "a creaturely feeling in the presence of Deity," we feel intuitively with Catherine Baird that this is as inadequate as declaring love to be an emotion or feeling known by one person concerning another. Like love, worship is an experience and cannot be adequately defined to those who have never known it.

Worship, as defined by Ralph P. Martin, is "the dramatic celebration of God in His supreme worth in such a manner that His worthiness becomes the norm and inspiration of human living." The goal of worship is the adoration of God for His own sake, and worship takes on authentic meaning only when God is at its heart. Yet its effects are felt throughout every aspect of our lives. Worship changes our attitude to God. It changes our conduct. It alters our sense of values. It affects our attitude to our work.

Fred Brown is a reliable guide when he writes in *The Salvationist at Prayer:* "The best way to deepen your spiritual life is to stop thinking of yourself and think far more of Him." Insisting that Salvationists must be Mary as well as Martha, Catherine Baird reminds us that "work and worship are partners but worship takes pride of place." It is sometimes said that conduct is supremely important and worship helps it. Not so, says William Temple. "The truth is that worship is supremely important and conduct tests it!" The outcome of worship is a desire to serve the one we worship.

Communal Worship

Fred Brown overstates his case when he asserts: "holy solitariness" is a phrase no more consistent with the gospel than "holy adulterers." Genuine worship as we know can be profoundly personal and private. He is a poor Salvationist who has never prayed in Albert Orsborn's words:

> In the secret of Thy presence,
> In the hiding of Thy power,
> Let me love Thee, let me serve Thee,
> Every consecrated hour.

Could any worship be more personal and private than that revealed in the words of Edward Joy:

Here I lay me at Thy bleeding feet,
Deepest homage now I give to Thee;
Hear Thy whispered love within my soul;
Jesus, Thou art everything to me!

Our primary concern here, however, is with communal worship. Although it might be argued persuasively that no particular times or places or forms of worship are obligatory for the Christian because God is Spirit and worship must be spiritual, it can be demonstrated quite clearly that, if such spiritual worship is to take place, our humanity requires that it take specific forms at set times in appropriate places.

Evelyn Underhill concludes from a study of history that it is the simple truth that "where this explicit embodiment is lacking and the Godward life of the community is not given some institutional expression, worship seldom develops its full richness and power. It remains thin, abstract and notional, a tendency, an attitude, a general aspiration, more alongside human life rather than in it." David Peck draws an analogy between a tree, the human body and the forms of worship. "The essence of an oak tree, that which gives to it its identity, its form, is conveyed by its characteristic leaf and shape. The essence of man, at the biological level, by the shape and appearance of the human body. So the forms and ceremonies of worship give shape and body to the movements of the Spirit." More directly, Tom Smail writes: "The Church should worship in the freedom that the Spirit gives, but also in a way that is an ordered reflection of the whole truth of the gospel as we have received it from Jesus Christ."

The life of the Early Church exhibits distinctive form, though not formalism, in its communal worship. Ralph Martin perceives three sides to early Christian worship: the charismatic side evidencing the power of the Holy Spirit; the didactic side expounding and explaining the truth as it is in Jesus; the eucharistic side in which Christians give thanks for the sacrifice of their Lord and Saviour. The New Testa-

139

ment, however, provides no detailed description of the external forms of Christian worship. The first Christians, it appears, adapted the forms of the synagogue insofar as they were compatible with their new faith in Christ. This freedom eventually succumbed to the expediency of established forms which inevitably led to empty formalism, which remains a problem to this day.

Salvationist Worship

Salvationists have not been exempt from the tendency to rely on forms, traditional structures and fixed liturgies in worship. Herein lies a tragedy. For no leader of public worship has more freedom than the Salvation Army officer. "No one is more free to be led of the Spirit than he who is responsible for conducting a Salvation Army meeting," writes General Frederick Coutts (R). "There is no liturgy he must follow. Apart from certain basic requirements such as prayer, Bible reading, personal testimony, a Bible address and the use of congregational singing, an officer is free to adopt any plans whatever, provided they are likely to accomplish the object in view and are in harmony with Bible teaching and with the spirit, practice and regulations of the Army."

This freedom led in the early days of our Movement to a rowdiness which bordered on irreverence. Salvationists were described as "like a rowdy company in a public house making games of religion." The Army "utterly vulgarizes the holiest things," it was stated, and "addresses called prayers were screamed out amidst the sound of dreadful drumming, the clangor of harsh instruments and shouts." Consequently, Salvationists have frequently found it necessary to defend their heritage against such charges.

In the Army hall, with its unpretentious appearance, there is little of the aesthetic that, in churches and cathedrals, holds us in its spell and helps us into an attitude of worship, but we have a sacred place, the penitent-form, where thousands of sinners have met with Christ and have made decisions that have changed their entire circumstances, perhaps costing all they have counted dear. Here the gifted young have consecrated education and all other privileges to the cause of Christ. Here all class and race barriers have disappeared and men and women, old and young, have united as children of one Father in His presence.

—Catherine Baird

Our meetings are as sacred—which does not mean dull or gloomy—as those held in any church or abbey. In them we come to God as truly as any who approach Him by means of high altar or communion table. In our meetings God's presence is invoked, His Word preached, His forgiveness offered, His grace received as freely and fully as where the air is charged with incense and rich with chanting.

—Frederick Coutts

Salvationists seeking deeper insight into their own heritage as a worshipping community will find much that is valuable in General Coutts' book, *In Good Company,* where chapters 22 to 25 are devoted to the worship of God. Not to be forgotten are the sections of *Orders and Regulations* which deal with public meetings. Helpful chapters on the holiness and salvation meetings and on public prayer are to be found in *The Salvationist at Worship,* by Fred Brown.

A question which arises as we worship in many of our corps concerns the price we have paid for our present respectability. Have the corps council's programs or the corps officer's priorities pre-empted the presence of the Holy Spirit? Has a blanket of uniformity smothered all initiative and spiritual freedom? Has the big blue machine taken over from its Lord and Master?

A fair evaluation of the meetings of The Salvation Army in Canada refutes such suggestions. For across our territory, there is demonstrated an incredible variety in public worship. A salvation meeting in Rocky Harbour has little similarity to a holiness meeting in London Citadel. A musicale at Earlscourt is quite a different affair from a congress in Prince Rupert. Even within the limits of Metropolitan Toronto,

Etobicoke Temple could not be mistaken for Greenwood. Nor could Kennedy Park and Agincourt, or Regent Park and North Toronto be confused with one another. The spirit of Salvationism which beats in the hearts of our comrades has many varied rhythms. Provided that this diversity manifests a true devotion to the Lord and a genuine Salvationism, let's praise the Lord for it!

Let the kindly counsel of General Coutts guide us not only in our relations with other believers, but also with fellow Salvationists:

> *I may not say to anyone who calls Jesus Lord—and none can do so save by the Spirit—your worship is defective. And, by the same token, nor may anyone say to me—because you have not taken part in this particular ceremony, you are none of His.*

"God is Spirit, and His worshippers must worship in spirit and in truth." They will most truly worship when, as the Lord's people, they open themselves to the guidance of His Spirit, allowing Him to lead them into the presence of the Heavenly Father.

Such worshippers the Father still seeks!